THE ART OF THE INTUITIVE HEALER

VOLUME 2

WAYNE LEE

A catalogue record of this book is available from the British Library.
ISBN 978-1-9999630-1-9

Editor: Angela Clarence
Typesetting/Book Design: Rising Sign Books
Cover design: Marc Thortnon at Digital Shift

TESTIMONIAL

I met Wayne through a healing group he runs and have never seen anyone work with energy the way that he did. I needed help releasing old negative emotions which felt deeply embedded – so much so that despite enormous efforts and trying various types of help, I thought perhaps I just wasn't capable of healing.

I have now had several sessions with Wayne and each session has been different but all have provided significant steps forward in my healing process. Because Wayne really, truly, accepts people as they are. It is so much easier to be open and honest about one's emotions and feelings. He doesn't judge, just uses his exceptional gift to then shift the negative stuff.

So, thank you Wayne. You do amazing things and I do feel very, very, lucky having your help.
Alice – UK

Wayne is an inspired healer. I've had sessions with him spanning a period of six years and every single one has been a powerful life-enhancing, life-changing event. When I recommend Wayne to friends and strangers, which I frequently do, I'm asked what exactly he does. Put most simply, he reconnects you to your essential self, the self that remembers life without trauma, fear, confusion, dis-ease. I come out of sessions feeling free, light and excited about my life.

During my first session I remember feeling a popping sensation all around my ribs- he told me it was trauma being released. He went on to explain how, in talk therapy, we are encouraged to understand trauma with our minds but that doesn't release it from our bodies, where it is stored. This made complete sense to me. Having had conventional therapy I was still experiencing limitations from the same issues I'd discussed over and over with a therapist.

Wayne uses a variety of techniques ranging from energy healing, visualisations, listening and communicating verbally, channeling and tapping. Guided by his ability to feel and see what is going on inside you, emotionally and energetically, you receive exactly what is needed in that session. There is no hiding from Wayne! You engage him as a healer when you're ready to see yourself as deeply as he sees you; when you're ready for real change and all the possibilities that that come with it. He's the most powerful facilitator of healing and transformation I've ever come across. I feel enormously grateful to have been introduced to him and to be able to continue having sessions with him.
Rebecca London UK

TABLE OF CONTENTS

Introduction

The process of becoming a confident, intuitive healer is amazing in itself, but when we allow the process to help us evolve, the potential to help others and ourselves is infinite. We learn to drop the boundaries that our lives, society, and teachers have taught us, so we can accept the fragility of our physical bodies, and make contact with the deepest part of our souls.

These changes are not about making us different people, but about revealing the true depth of our loving and caring power. We can only love others as much as we love ourselves. So it is vital to discover our internal love, delve deep into that love and accept ourselves as we are in our perfect imperfect uniqueness, banishing any fears of exposing the vulnerable, loving souls that we are.

It is a process that is never-ending, and while I have mastered these skills to some degree, I have only just begun to scratch the surface of the depth of love and acceptance available to share with myself, my family, friends, clients, the world and the entire universe.

You will come to your own conclusions as to how best the tools I am offering will work for you. You can use them in many ways: to heal yourself and your clients; to increase self-love; for inspiration and personal development; for healing family issues and so much more. The boundaries of loving are limitless.

THE THREE BASIC ASPECTS

The art of being an intuitive healer covers three fundamental aspects of healing and self-mastery. The practice of being at one with yourself physically, mentally and energetically with total acceptance, allows the universe to become the teacher. Who would you rather have as your teacher, someone who has learned second-hand information from someone else, or your higher self, your guides and the universe?

We need to be present in the centered flow of our body, mind, and energy. If one of these components is not present, we are not allowing the healing to be our teacher and offer its full potential. We are not allowing the universe to feed and flow through us. If we are not present with ourselves, we cannot be present for our clients.

The three aspects have an order which works for me, and I believe will also work for most people, but once you have mastered the oneness they bring, you will have the universe to help you find your own way.

However, even if we are not totally balanced, it doesn't mean we should stop seeing clients. No, not at all. Clients come to see us because they need to learn to recognise their own love just as much as we do. Our process is also their process. Their process is also our process. We cannot separate ourselves from our clients because we are all 'one'. So don't stop seeing clients. Trust more and work on discovering your love more. It is most likely the fear of being in connection with ourselves, that is preventing us from connecting fully with our own love. So as I said, trust more and allow the healing to be the most important part of the process - beyond our needs and the needs of the client.

***

Firstly, as we are humans in a human world on this earth plane, we need to start off with the physical. We have to respect the earth and all living things on the earth. We have to accept that we are on this planet and that death is ours to fear or revere, ours to deny or accept. We have to live a life of certain death. The only certainty in our physical world is death, so when you accept that, you start to let go of one of the biggest boundaries of life. Fear of death and the unknown can hold you back, and so your intuition cannot find its flow. I am not asking you to be suicidal, or push your physical body beyond its earthly ability. I am asking you to let go of the fear of being wrong. To let go of any need to understand everything. I am asking you to go for it, to take the leap and trust yourself as a mortal, fallible human, and to trust yourself more and more.

Secondly, as naturally intuitive animals, we have to accept our influential mind and start to master our thoughts. We have to accept that the mind and its thoughts are not who we are and that our minds can often be our biggest enemies. We need to re-programme negative, self-belittling thoughts with thoughts of loving gentleness towards ourselves. What we are thinking when we are healing is the key which opens the door to flowing, organic, universal love and healing. **We must be gentle with ourselves.**

Thirdly, we are souls in a physical body; we are not a body with a soul, our energy is the true essence of who we are. Our physical and mental aspects are also just energy. Energy is love. Love is the healer. Offer your genuine love, and you are offering the power of the universe, the same power the 'universe' would use to create worlds of life just like our beloved home.

We must combine the open connection to our physical bodies, go clarity of mind, and to our love. Accept these three parts as 'one', and then we can allow ourselves to be the universal healing channel between our love, ourselves and our clients. Offering the purest of love helps people heal beyond our limitations and expectations.

This process is not a quick fix. It is not easy as we are heavily programmed to disconnect from our love. So let us be gentle with ourselves during this enlightening process. We will not beat ourselves up or doubt ourselves. Instead, we will be kind and nurturing and swim through the lake of patience as if it is the source of all love itself.

PART ONE
PHYSICAL HEALING

CHAPTER ONE - BREATHING

The first aspect of being a productive and powerful intuitive healer is the connection to your physical self. If you are not in touch with your physical human self, you are going to be a slower channel of energy and inspiration than you can be when you are more connected to your body. We are humans on the earth plane and must respect the reality of our human life. In the womb, we go through the process of being physically created but are still very much the spiritual energetic being we were in the universal energy of the spirit energy planes.

As soon as we are released from our mother's womb, our first job is to learn to breathe. Then we start to become aware of our bodies and learn movement, and physical connection in our earth gravity lives. Physical awareness is the first step to being a connected, complete human being. Our physical bodies make us the human beings that we are in the heavy thick atmosphere of the earth plane, and breathing is an essential skill for our survival. Even though it is built into our DNA, many of us unlearn the natural method of breathing.

Getting in touch with your physical self is an ongoing process that always starts with the building block of life that is breathing. If you are breathing correctly, which means using your full range of breath, you are much more connected to your body. The breath connects you to your root, to your primal natural instinct as a human and is always the first step to being grounded and 'in the moment'. Focusing on breathing pulls you into the moment. It allows you to focus on yourself as you are right now and takes you away from disconnected thoughts about past and future. Breathing pulls you into the now, into the present, which is the essence of being grounded. Which includes both the physical and the inner space that you are in every moment of every day. So the awareness of what is happening in the now is not just about standing in your kitchen, but also about how you feel, and what you are experiencing while standing in your kitchen, no matter whether it is comfortable or challenging.

To improve your breath/body connection follow your breath with your mind to check if you are using the full range of your lungs or not. If not, you can re-educate yourself to breathe more efficiently.

As you breathe to connect to yourself some of you will notice that you are snatching your breath (in fear), are shallow breathing (taking fast panting breaths), or have a skip in your breath (like a slight hiccup as you breathe). Most of us breathe faster and shallower than we should, but with focus, we can learn to slow our breathing down to a natural breathing flow. On the other hand, taking huge deep breaths that make you shift your physical body will pull you out of connection with yourself. So focussing on your natural range of breath is important.

1 - Breathing In

To breathe correctly first take the air into the bottom of your lungs. Filling your lungs up from the bottom is like pouring water into a glass from the bottom up and is the perfect way to re-educate your breathing.

2 - Breathing Out

Breathing out is just as important as breathing in! On the out-breath push the air out from the bottom of your lungs - like squeezing the bottom of the tooth paste tube. In doing this, you fully empty your lungs so that the next breath will be an entirely new one. I use the out-breath as a release as it pushes the pressure or stress out of my body helping it to relax.

Try taking 5 or 6 breaths and focus on the out-breath as much as you focus on the in-breath. Be aware of how it makes you feel to breathe out and how it reacts in your body. Just learning to do this will connect you with a part of yourself you may never have considered before. Keep in mind that the out-breath is a release from the past and so is a step forward in your life. In this way, we let go of the past and accept the future! The in breath is the acceptance of life, and the out breath is the preparation for life.

3 - Breathing and Fear

If you watch a baby breathe, there is a short interval af-ter the baby's out-breath when the infant is waiting for its body to control its breathing and then the body gives a defined signal for it to inhale slowly and naturally. That is the natural way to breathe. Often, when parents watch their baby breathing and notice that pause, they think that their baby isn't breathing and get anxious and that anxiety can instil fear in the child which causes an instinctive shallowing in its breath. I have had to remind thousands of clients to take a breath on releasing a trauma because their body instinctively shallows its breath when fear or trauma is actively shifting in the body.

4 - Visualisation

When advancing your breathing, the tool of visualisation is the key to success. Try visualising the air going in and out of your lungs as you breathe, taking your mind with you on your breathing journey will help you to get a better understanding of how your breathing is changing.

You can also work on connecting the breath to different parts of the body. Try visualising breathing into your feet; into individual chakras; head; eyes; mouth; neck; and shoulders. Use the full capacity of your lungs filling from bottom to top, connecting to those different parts. It's quite a profound experience that I really enjoy, especially breathing into the bridge of my nose. Releasing the bridge of the nose will release the eyes and the cheeks and will also begin to release the jaw; an area that many of us are unaware is under stress.

As you breathe to connect to yourself, don't try and stretch your lungs as that will distract you from actually connecting to yourself. Taking huge deep breaths that make you shift your physical body will pull you out of connection with yourself. So focussing on your natural range of breath is important. For anyone who has never focused on their breathing, the following exercises are tools that can be used every day, in all areas of your life, but they are not a quick fix - you have to practice!

5 - Five Breaths to Self-Connection

'The Five Breaths' is a method I have created out of Tai Chi because of a smidgen of fear of not being able to connect to myself within the practicalities of a busy working family life. It is a technique that brings the physical body into a space that is ready to connect with both mental and energy bodies.

Within a minute, I can take the five breaths slowly, and add 4 or 5 breaths at the end to experience moving towards my true power.

a. Centre Yourself

- On your first breath bring your mind down to the bottom of your lungs
- Focus on the air going in and out from the bottom and breathe the full range of your lungs
- Focus on connecting your mind with your breath
- The in-breath connects you to your body and says I am here now
- The out-breath releases your body and says I accept the now, and makes space and acceptance for the next moment

b. Ground Yourself

- On the in-breath visualise your feet stretching and reaching toward the floor - visualise them reaching down and away from the body and connecting with the earth
- As you release the out-breath accept the flow of life

c. Universal Connection
- When you breathe in, reach down with your feet at the same time as reaching up with the crown chakra - the top of your head stretching up to the sky - your body is elongating, connecting with both the earth and the sky
- On the out-breath accept your human self

d. Accepting your Power
- Visualise the bottom of your lungs as the centre point of the body
- On the in-breath visualise your entire body expanding out from that centre, your body is one big balloon, and as you breathe into the balloon the entire body expands outwards in all directions
- On the out-breath release yourself and your expectations

e. Earth Bound Experiencing
- Now on the in-breath accept yourself in the moment. Continue accepting your true self in this moment for as long as you like. If you get distracted, acknowledge the distraction and refocus on your centre and your breath
- Allow your body to experience your true self in connection with humanity and the universal energy just for the length of each breath

The 5 Breaths is a great tool to get you connected to your body. I suggest you do it as often as you can. When you become practiced at it, you will become skilled at centering your physical body. You will be able to do it in only a few moments, but to get there you will have to practice!

The best way I have found to practice is to centre yourself before opening a door. Every door! Before you open the fridge, centre yourself. Before you open the front door centre yourself, before you open the car door, before you open the cupboard to get a biscuit. There is no rush, but you will see changes in just a few days. Clients have reported changes in feeling safe, more motivated, having a stronger sense of self, as well as a marked change in eating habits. When they connect to themselves before opening a cupboard or the fridge, they avoid uncontrolled subconscious eating!

Learning to breathe correctly in connection to yourself is an essential life tool but teaching your body how to break old breathing habits and replace them with powerful new ones needs to be practiced. So practice! Practice is the order of the day.

In conclusion, it makes no matter which way you choose to improve your breathing; it is the focussing on your breath that is important! If you just sit and watch yourself breathe in and out, your primal energetics will slowly start to bring your breathing into its natural range. It is taking the time to stop and focus on yourself that creates the change.

Chapter Two – Hands

As healers, our hands are one of the most important tools of our trade, and I had taken for granted that my hands would just know what to do without any input from me. Oh boy, was I wrong!

We need to exercise our hands, just as we need to stretch before we prepare our bodies to run a marathon. We need to stretch our hands to allow them to open energetically. We need to focus on how they are functioning and listen to them as we are working. Just as we listen to our bodies as to when to push ourselves and when to rest, so we must do the same for our hands.

I hear a client's body through my hands, but it is the awareness of my hands that allows me to feel, hear, sense and connect to them. Our hands can give us important messages into what is happening both for us and our clients. So learn to exercise them and practice! Practice! Practice! Practice!

Over the years I have been teaching I have heard some incredible stories from apprentice healers. My favourite is that of a student who was told that if his fingers were not together healing would stop! Another had been taught that thumbs needed to be tucked close to fingers with hands curved. Also, that if their hands became flat the energy would be blocked. Another had socks put on their hands and was told that when their fingers were open enough to stretch the socks flat that that was the correct position for healing! (I had an image of healers in bare feet with socks on their hands)!

What works for one may not work for another, but it is important that you hold your hands in a way that feels most natural and comfortable to you.

To be more connected to your hands it is important to know a little about the energy of the hands and arms:

If you stand up and let your hands fall to the side of your body, your hands will naturally hang in your base chakra energy, so your hands and wrists are a base chakra grounding energy.

Equally, your 'forearms' are sacral chakra energy, your 'elbows' are solar plexus energy, 'upper arms' are heart chakra, 'shoulders and neck' are throat chakra energy and your skull and temples relate to your third eye energy.

Through our arms, we are channelling an extensive range of chakra energy, and our hands are the grounding of that range of healing energy. The chakra in the palm and the chakras in the fingers and thumbs are all base chakra related and are focused on grounding. We are channelling the universal energy of healing through our bodies and using our hands as the grounding of the energy.

When we are offering energy healing, we are completing the circuit of energy through our body by grounding the excess flow of energy into the client's body. This in-turn starts the client's energy moving as a reaction to our flow of energy. As we allow energy flow, their energy flows because 'like creates like.' We are influencing the healing process through the client's body. So it is vital to be at one with ourselves, connected to the highest vibration and as centred as possible in a healing session.

After working with many clients in a day, my hands sometimes swell to the point that I struggle to bend my fingers during a session and I believe it's the Chi energy waiting to be used. Within a half-an-hour after the session, my hands return to normal.

Hand Awareness and Exercises

Some of these exercises which I have adapted to assist healing abilities came from my Tai Chi experiences.

1 – Stretching the Palm Chakra

If you run your finger around the centre of your palm, you will feel a defined difference between the bone and ligaments and the soft misshaped circle area - this soft part is your palm chakra.

Hold your hands gently out in front of you and allow your mind to be aware of how they feel. You will probably feel healing begin to flow just because you are focusing on your palm chakra.

To stretch open the chakra imagine that the outer tip of your thumb is slightly spiralling away from your hand turning the thumb outward and opening up away from your palm. At the same time focus on your middle finger and imagine it is getting slightly longer, also moving away from your palm.

Do not physically try and move the thumb and finger; that would be forcing the chakra open and will not benefit you. Visualisation allows the thumb to twist away and open up, and the middle finger stretch away with only a small physical movement on your hands.

Once you feel the energy in your palm chakra, you should also feel an increase in energy and a stiffness creeping into the joints of your hand as the chakras open all the way through the palm and fingers. Opening the palm causes the rest of the chakras in the hand to open also. The stiffness is just the joints naturally aligning themselves.

Now spend a minute or two allowing your mind to be present with your hands, and experience the feeling of your chakras stretching open.

After performing this exercise, I rub my palms together which closes the chakras back down.

Exercise your palms once or twice a day or for 10-20 seconds before offering healing. Before you know it, this will become automatic for you.

2 - Chi Dripping

Chi dripping is a fantastic exercise for removing any stiffness or pain from your neck all the way down to your fingertips, and also a preventative to neck pains and stiffness due to stress or repetitive strain injuries. It also works well for shoulder, elbow and wrist pain and is the exercise I offer to people with frozen shoulders as a key to releasing the blocked energy.

Find a space where you can to let your hands hang unhindered by your sides either standing or sitting on a chair. Find your centre by breathing as per The Five Breaths. Allow your arms to hang naturally by your sides and imagine that your fingers are getting a little longer, at the same time visualising your crown chakra lifting to the sky. See the energy from the very top of your neck running down the inside and outside of your arms, through the bone, muscle, and skin. When the energy reaches your hand, let it stretch off your long fingers and drip onto and into the ground. Check your neck and shoulders and release them, letting them hang down and stretch to the ground. Allow the release and keep focusing on the chi dripping from your fingers. You should feel a stretch in the muscles of your neck and shoulders when you have released the muscles sufficiently. I find that clients often need to do this several times before they feel the stretch.

I like to practice this exercise daily for 2 or 3 minutes using a stopwatch.

3 - Energy Balls

Put your hands out gently in front of you and create an energy ball between your palms and focus on the energy in your hands. Be aware of how your hands feel while holding the energy. Visualise stretching and shaping the ball. Learning how the energy flows through you and shaping it will be of benefit to your work. Try splitting your hands and holding an energy ball in each hand and then reconnecting them together. Healing energy naturally pools together like water and the increasing energy you are holding will, in turn, help the chakra in the hands to open up. I even create small energy balls between my thumb and fingers to exercise the chakras in the fingertips. In conclusion, thank and appreciate the hands and offer them respect and love. They are an important part of our lives as healers and humans.

4 – Reiki Attunements

Reiki came to the West just before the Second World War and since then it has been passed on to millions of people to the benefit of many. I love Reiki, and for me, it was the first step to my new self. I was lucky enough to be able to use my intuition to understand the process of the attunement to Reiki, and my ability to see energy has helped me when I attune students and due to this I have found myself re-attuning hundreds of hands over the years.

I was running a workshop on Advanced Intuitive Healing a few years ago and the students were practicing healing on each other so that I could see what was happening energetically. When one of the ladies put her hands on her recipient I couldn't see any energy movement from her hands at all. I asked if she could feel energy moving through her hands but when she said she wasn't sure I asked her about her healing journey. She told me that she had been attuned to healing as a level 2 Reiki. I told her that I felt that she wasn't actually healing to the full potential she had available and asked if I could re-attune her hands. She readily agreed - the process only takes moments when you have done it hundreds of times before, as I have. I also checked her body attunement which felt fine and within a few minutes of returning to her recipient she was aware that her hands "were different" and that all of a sudden she could indeed feel the movement of energy going through her hands. Her friend, who had been attuned by the same Reiki Master asked me to check her hands and they also needed to be re-attuned and the chakras fully opened.

Some healers teaching Reiki tend to repeat what they have been taught as a blind ritual, without feeling or understanding the process, and when I have taught Attuning Workshops, I have seen many Reiki Masters wake-up to the fact that they have not been attuning correctly. When it is done properly and with the correct intention and knowledge it becomes very empowering and beautiful for the Master. Actually it is more wonderful for the Master than the receiver as the Master should be more energetically aware than the student.

Chapter Three – The Body

1 - Trusting the Twitches

Sensations in your own body can be pointers as to what is going on for your client. When I am working, I keep as much awareness of what is happening to my own physical body as I do theirs. I often get an itch, a touch, a bump, or the odd shooting pain or cramp during a session. I check in with myself, and if I have no reason to be itching or experiencing a different sensation in that area of my body, I often move my hand and focus on that spot on the client's body. After a short while, if the sensation hasn't gone away, I try the exact opposite side of my client's body because the sensation might have polarised onto the opposite side when it was communicating with me and wait to see if it clears. Very often that point is precisely relevant to the client's healing process.

These prompts can come from a spiritual guide, or intuitive source that has poked my body to make me aware of what is needed for the client's highest good or they can also be feedback from the client's trauma that needs to be recognized and is bouncing off of my energy.

A specific example of this occurred one day when greeting a regular client at the door; I was aware of a dull, itching feeling in my right ear. I scratched at it, rubbed it and tapped it. When it continued to bug me, I asked my client if there was an issue with her right ear. She told me that she had had a recurring ear infection in her left ear and hadn't mentioned it as she was taking medication. I told her that the left ear could either relate to a fear of what people were saying about her, or to her not being heard. When she said that the explanation fitted we worked on her fear of what might happen if she were to be heard. We worked through her fear of being herself and the issue getting into trouble as a child when she had wanted to be heard.

My awareness of my physical self had not only helped to reinforce the healing session but also augmented her trust in me and my ability to help her.

2 – Hui Yin

This exercise is about centering, and being aware of your energetics, and the flows of energy that are working through your body. The thought and intention of fully connecting to yourself will automatically increase the amount of energy you can channel; and as your healing vibration increases, so too will your ability to connect to higher levels of spiritual vibration and inspiration. It is also important to remember that while healing flows through you, it does not and must not come from your personal energy.

The Hui Yin exercise serves to increase the flow of healing by connecting two of the main meridians in your body: the central and governing channels. Hui Yin brings together the front and back of the body - the past and the present - bringing you into the grounded "now" of life and reinforcing your flow in the moment.

The front meridian connects to your past and any energy you may be holding from your past. It is the central meridian that runs through your base chakra at your perineum (between your anus and genitals) connecting with the pubic bone flowing up the front of your body through the belly button to the bottom lip and through to the tip of your tongue.

The back meridian connects to your future and anxiety about future events. It is the governing meridian which runs from your perineum through your coccyx, up along the centre of your spine, over the back of your head and ends just in front of your upper canine teeth below your nose.

To connect these two meridians, contract your perineum while placing the tip of your tongue on the roof of your mouth just behind your front teeth.

When using this method, do not force the perineum closed by clenching too hard on your buttocks as this will distract you from your healing. Practice by slowly tightening your perineum and touching your tongue to your pallet, imagining that a cord is attached to your perineum and flows through the middle of the body via your navel and up to your mouth.

Becoming aware of the Hui Yin meridians and practising this exercise while meditating and healing will help you to master this skill, and you'll find it begins to happen automatically. At times while I am working with a client I become aware that my tongue is twisted weirdly pushing up on my pallet as my guides are trying to bring me more into my centre to be able to use more chanelled energy.

3 - Your Comfort First, Your Clients' Comfort Second

There is no point in hurting yourself to help your clients, so make sure that you are not standing, bending or sitting in an awkward position when you are working. The client will be with you for around an hour through an average session, but if you may well find yourself seeing five or more in a day, and that's a long time to be uncomfortable. Your comfort comes first, so make sure that you have got all you need to be comfortable which may include water, food, clothing, and chairs. If you use a healing couch, make sure it is at the right height for you and that you have a step available for disabled or shorter clients so you that you don't hurt yourself helping them on or off the couch. While I care about my client's comfort, I don't jeopardise my needs for theirs.

At one charity event, I gave 38 twenty-minute healing sessions over two days. If I had not been comfortable from the start things would have got progressively worse, and I would have been distracted from the connection to myself and not been a clear channel for the clients. I sometimes take 6-day healing trips which include 10 hours of travelling, 6 hours of workshops, and 37 one-hour healing sessions. That's a lot of work in 6 days! So focussing on the right seating, the right healing couch height, water intake, healthy food, and plenty of sleep is essential. I also try and make sure that when I get home, I take a few days to recover, making space for myself.

Be aware of what you are wearing and how it may affect your client. Might your jewellery get caught on their hair or clothing? Could your clothes be brushing over the client's body? Is the clinking of your jewellery causing the client to be less relaxed? Healers can sometimes be flamboyant, presenting ourselves with crystals and rings and bangles and studs etc. but be aware that while these may make you feel comfortable and represent your beliefs, it might be wise to remove them while you work.

One of the members of my Intuitive Healing Development Group loves big bulky crystal pendants and wears them proudly. While bending over a female client, I saw his pendant rubbing her body close to an inappropriate position. I pointed out that without him even knowing it his pendant could be a lawsuit waiting to happen! It's easy to get caught up in the process of being 'spiritual', of 'being a healer', but it might be making you less effective.

4 - Accepting your Physical Self

Acceptance is one of the big keys to everything we do in our lives. You have to accept yourself before you can accept others. When you are accepting a client as perfect and allowing them to change, because you accept them, it's possible that your own limitations can affect the outcome.

If you don't accept the way you look, your anger, or that it's ok to doubt yourself, those parts feel rejected, are disconnected from the self, which decreases the level of energy you can channel. If you ignored your right arm for a few years - never accepted it and even rejected using it – your arm would wither away and become a burden. When you accept your arm and use it with love and nurture, it becomes a strong and important part of your life. So it is with all the parts, be they physical, emotional or mental.

If you are not working on accepting your true human self - the good and what we deem to think of as the bad parts of ourselves - the universe will keep bringing clients to who are not allowing growth in their lives – clients with the same issues! Round and around you go, not accepting yourselves, but as a healer you have to understand how important it is to heal and grow in your own acceptance because if you don't, you will find yourself blocking the healing of your clients. If you cannot evolve, then neither can your clients.

It is hard to be totally self-accepting, and I don't put that kind of harsh pressure on myself, or expect it of anyone else. However, it is extremely powerful just to recognise that there are parts of our physical, emotional and spiritual selves about which we are unhappy and would like to change. That is, in itself, a way of accepting yourself. You are not putting yourself down. You are accepting what you see as an issue - an unsatisfactory part of yourself. Acknowledging that you would like to change it is the first step to self-acceptance, it cuts out the self-doubt, discontinues old self-deprecating patterns and is a wonderful tool to share with your clients.

I have had a life long struggle with my weight spending thousands of hours putting myself down and creating even more issues for myself. Over the past five years, I have managed to change the pattern and acknowledge my weight as a grand, priceless tool to help me grow. I know for a fact that I would not be the healer I am now if I had been slender. I remember the day I realised that I had been telling my body it was bad for being fat - a pattern taught by my mother. Her inability to accept herself or me and her worry about my weight created this negative self-belittling belief about my body. I remember sitting and meditating and speaking to my body one day. I asked it for forgiveness; I gave it love. I said I was sorry. I said thank you for its help, even though I was blaming it for my shortcomings. I remember very clearly how 'angry' my body was with me and how much lighter I felt after I acknowledged my body's right to be angry with me. I recognised that I was not taking responsibility for myself at a soul level and had been blaming my body. I was not allowing my body to receive love from my soul. I also worked on accepting my anger toward my mother, and offered her love and understanding, recognising that she too was but a product of her childhood.

I have found that many of us fight connection to their pain, disease or illness which we try to make invisible by ignoring or medicating the problem - the very opposite of what we should be doing. I believe we should try and understand why 'it' is there and what 'its' message is for us. We should take our minds down into the part of our body that is in distress and try and be with it and look at what we can learn from this dis-ease.

It is also extremely important to recognise that many of us have brought disease into our human lives as a way of learning - as a part of their path in this incarnation.

I had a client who had skin cancer. She had a huge tumour on her right shoulder (golf ball size), very horrid looking and violent in appearance. She kept it well hidden and couldn't bear to look at it herself. When she told me about the tumour, I asked if I might see it and then reached out and caressed it gently. Her entire body went into a trauma shock release. I was the first person who had ever touched it without first putting on gloves. Everyone else, even the doctors, found it hard to touch with nurture. I asked her to start a daily regime of speaking to it with love, stroking it with affection and giving it healing. Before the tumour was removed, I wanted this area to feel loved, to create a place of loving energy for the skin and flesh to regrow without the dis-ease.

I believe our soul tries its very best to communicate with us. It makes us feel happy and elated when things are good and balanced, and we appreciate this. It makes us feel pain and unease and illness when it is trying to communicate that things are not as good or balanced as they could be, but we tend to disconnect and ignore this! If we have been ignoring our soul's communication for a very long time, it becomes desperate and creates a dis-ease that we cannot ignore - although many of us do not recognise the message. Instead, we give up responsibility for our personal well-being to a doctor, who is entirely unconnected to what is going on with our body and soul resulting in two people ignoring what the soul needs!

What our body needs is for us to STOP (yes, stop!) stop doing, stop going, stop pushing. It needs us to stop and listen. Listen to what we are feeling. Listen to what is making us unhappy or unbalanced. When you have listened you can acknowledge what is happening in your body and acknowledgment is the first step to change

Part of being a healer is to stop, listen and connect to the client so that they get both heard and seen.

I recall a client who came to me for help with his obsessive compulsive disorder (OCD). Over several sessions, we worked on his need for feeling safe and his inability to process his emotions. On his seventh or eighth session, we did some work on his lack of emotional release. After discussions, we worked on allowing him to be angry. At his next session he said he wanted to go back to how he had been before the last session because he had been angry with everyone all week. He had even found himself screaming at his parents which had never done before. He said: "I would rather have my OCD than feel this anger."

At that moment I knew he could get control of his OCD - he had accepted it because he was willing to choose it over his anger. I convinced him to let his anger run for another week. I suggested that he should go to his parents and apologise for taking his anger out on them, but must 'never apologise for being angry'. I explained that it was OK to let his anger out. That all emotions are important and if he needed to apologise for being angry, then he needed to apologise for being happy and every other emotion!

Over the following few weeks his anger diminished and his need to be compulsive lessened. His world changed even more when he found himself in a relationship. He had begun to move forward in his life. On his last session, he told me that he was still using his OCD habits when he felt unsafe, but it was now a tool and that it no longer controlled his life. The acceptance of his OCD had been the major step in changing his illness. As soon as he had accepted that part of himself, it had started to shift. Awareness is key.

Accepting all our parts is essential. While accepting ourselves is common sense, putting it into practice takes work! It takes courage and patience to work through our 'stuff' and truly accept ourselves. When you start on this journey, you will find your whole life opens up to new and wonderful lessons and will bring new, wonderful, open people into your world. Yes, it's hard work, but as healers, I believe it is essential and worth the striving. We are just as much in need of healing and it is a wonderful way of learning how to help others.

5 - Everything is Relevant in a Healing Session

As it says in the title, everything is relevant when you are in a healing session. Your Guides, higher self, spirit family, and helpers will try and communicate in any way that they can. As an intuitive healer, you need to be open enough to feel, see, and accept everything that happens as a possible relevant snippet of information to help you understand and help your client.

I use what I call shallow vision. When I work with a client, I bring my eyesight back - slightly out of focus, and as broad as possible - so I am aware of much more than just looking at my client. I watch the windows, walls, and flickers of movement with my eyes, I listen to everything with my ears, and I feel everything with my entire body. I am seeking any information that comes through; no matter how trivial I may think it is. I hold that information, and if it's relevant, it will keep coming up, or keep showing itself to me.

I also listen with my body, I hear the client, and I am aware of every word, but only the words that I feel in my body will I hold in my memory. I feel my client's words and allow the emotions that they trigger to be a part of the messages I am receiving for my client. This listening is a technique that is easy to practice and needs practice. Listen to your family and friends in the normal way, but also open your body up to listen to their words. Then recognise what emotions are triggering in your emotional body, acknowledge them and check how they make you feel and then reflect on what that means to you.

I also feel with my memories. When a client is with me and communicating their issues - their sadness or their illness - I allow their feelings to wash over me, reflecting on what they are feeling through memories of my feelings. Feeling my client's feelings triggers personal memories of feelings similar to those of my clients. I have not felt every feeling that is possible, but many of the emotions my clients are experiencing will be in my emotional memory bank. When those memories come to me, I can use them to understand more of what is happening with my client, to understand my clients beyond what they can recognise in themselves and so aid them even more in their healing process. If I get a sense of sadness or betrayal in a client who has no idea why they have an illness or problem, I can use the information to establish a foundation to work from.

For instance, sadness is a solar plexus chakra response, so I can start by connecting to their solar plexus.

Betrayal is a trauma and thus would be a sacral chakra trauma response, so I know to look at their sacral chakra as a place to work.

The ability to allow everything that happens in a session is enormously relevant and is a wonderful tool to have in the intuitive healer's repertoire.

A client told me on an initial contact call that she was desperate to see me and booked the first space I had available. When she arrived, I could feel she was in severe emotional trauma. She told me her career was important to her and that she had recently lost her job due to an issue with her direct senior; and that the owner who should have been backing her up after 14 years of working with him and becoming good friends, had let her down. She was in the process of legal proceedings against the previous employer because of being illegally dismissed, but she hadn't been able to sleep for months because of the anger she felt. Her new boss had suggested she come to me to help get rid of the anger.

As she spoke, I could feel her feelings, and it triggered a memory of the feelings I had had when a partner had cheated on me in the past. The severe feeling of being betrayed flooded my body, and I saw it as important and relevant information. I looked at her and said, "I think that your anger is attached to your initial reaction to the situation, but I don't think you are actually angry any more, it's just that you can't process the real feelings you are having." She reacted aggressively and jumped at me crying, "I AM ANGRY!"

I said calmly "It could it be that you are feeling the anger as a response to feeling hurt and betrayed." She stopped for a moment, the energy in her body dropped, the anger melted away, as emotional pain took its place, and she cried. She hadn't recognised that she felt deeply hurt over the betrayal by her boss and that she was not actually angry anymore.

When her emotional release subsided, I explained that anger is a passionate response to the deeply buried feeling of being hurt and that she had been unable to recognise the hurt and betrayal by her previous boss and ex-friend.

I have had sessions where a common fly will arrive in the room. Even though the doors and windows are closed, in comes a fly to pester us, and it is always relevant. It usually means that my client is being pestered, or festering on something unnecessarily. If I am talking to a client and an unusual noise occurs, I also take it as relevant to the session.

For the first time in the three years working in my healing room, a man began to strim the lawn opposite my house with a petrol strimmer. The noise it made was so loud that my client and I couldn't hear each other. We had to wait until he finished his extremely thorough strimming which took ages. My client was obviously irritated, but I waited quietly and patiently and when the noise finally stopped I said, "So not being heard no matter how much noise you make, irritates, frustrates and angers you and you have no idea how to change that." She went silent, and tears started to roll down her cheeks. The universe had brought us that man so that we didn't have to beat around the bush finding out what was going on for her. We knew where to start working.

Be open to allowing the universe to help in your sessions.

CHAPTER FOUR – CHAKRA AWARENESS

It is important to learn about your energy field understanding the individual chakras, how they work, how you can work with them and how to create your own language for your energy and your chakras.

Although chakras are an 'energetic' part of our bodies, we have to start working with our chakras in conscious, physical ways. We need to allow our body to increase its vibration so that our soul can be open enough to connect to a greater volume of universal energy - which vibrates at a much higher rate than our physical body. When we are grounded, and in our breath, we create a far more stable platform to connect and channel that universal vibration.

The only true way for you to come to an understanding of what chakras mean to you, and how they work and affect you and your clients, is for you to experience the energy of your chakras in your day-to-day life. Learning to open and close your chakras and spending time connecting to each chakra are an essential part of your energy awareness. So it is important to check in with yourself during the day to see how you are feeling emotionally, physically and energetically with the intention of understanding your chakra state at that moment.

Early in my career I recall a client coming to see me because she had been told by several healers that her repetitive throat infections were caused by a blocked throat chakra. She could feel the chakra was clear when she was receiving healing but within a few hours it felt as if it had closed again with a feeling as if something was stabbing her throat giving her sharp, random pains.

So I focused on her throat chakra, but held my intuition open for inspiration. I had placed my right hand on throat but became aware that my left hand wanted to go to her sacral chakra and as I connected on to the flow of energy in it, I became aware of a change in my right hand. Working on her sacral chakra was affecting the pull of energy on her throat chakra. I let go of her throat chakra and found myself gliding my right hand over her sacral chakra energy - like a hawk gliding on an air thermal. I did this for some time, and kind of got lost in the energy of feeling her sacral chakra energy. I became aware that the vibration did not feel right, it was out of sync, and was held in a trauma state. The feeling reminded me of how I feel when I connect to my own traumas - especially around being bullied. I started to feel several different vibrations within this single chakra and became aware that each different feeling was a different trauma vibration. With all this information filling my awareness I became a little lost on what to do with this knowledge.

All I knew, deep in my core, was the trust I have in my guidance and inspiration, so I opened myself up to allow my guides and inspiration to show me what to do. I let go of trying to work it out, reconnected to my breath, opened my chakras further, and then waited, waited for my guides to show me the way.

I lost control over my hand's movements as my guide took over. My fingertips came together making a point and my hand dipped into the chakra and then dived through the vortex of the chakra. As I reached close to her body, my fingers flared wide open again. With my hand spread wide open the sense of vibration was now all over my hand and it felt like I was trying to pull her entire body up off the bed by just using her auric field. I realised that I was actually pulling on her sacral chakra's energy. The pulling sensation was sending vibrations and light shooting pains up my arm which made me think of the pain she would experience in her throat. I thought I was not strong enough to pull this energy out of her chakra and just then in my mind I heard "let go!" So I focused on my breath, and I let go. All of a sudden my hand was lifting higher and higher and then my hand was shaking in alignment with the vibration of releasing the chakra. As I pulled her blocked chakra out of her body, releasing the trauma as I went along, her reaction was that of shock! She felt strange sensations all over her body and her eyes and mouth were open wide, and she said she felt herself become very light.

My guide was still in control of my arms, and my right hand swept across the chakra and pulled on the energetics clearing it with a sense of a 'rip'. It felt as if I was releasing any remnants of trauma from the chakra. Then both my hands were on her sacral chakra giving it clean, fresh universal energy for it to use to recreate its natural vortex and to heal itself.

I stood there, very quiet, asking my guides for more guidance on what I had just learned. I had experienced the feeling of a chakra and how it worked.

By practicing and letting inspiration and intuition into my healing session, I had started the process of understanding how chakras work for me.

From that one session I learned:
- that chakras hold energetic blocks - they can hold thousands of energetic blocks.
- that you can glide on a chakra.
- that you can enter a chakra.
- that you can pull and release the trauma in a chakra.
- that I could create change by being in-tune with my chakra and my client's chakra.
- that when a throat chakra is blocked, it is most likely the sacral chakra that is causing this block.

Over the years I have realised that people who have been bullied, or who have suffered aggression and so have not been 'allowed to be' develop this double chakra trauma. If you are being bullied, the sacral chakra will hold the trauma, but while you are being bullied and the bully is not listening to you, when you say "Stop!", "Go away!" or "No!" it then affects your throat chakra.

All this has given me tools to understand how to help thousands of people.

Here are some basic concepts that I have learned over the years about chakras that help me every day while I work with clients. I am listing them for you to keep in your awareness so that you can discover if the information is right for you or not.

Your chakras are communicating with you, your higher self, your guides, and other people's chakras every moment of every day. It's up to you to listen and to acknowledge them.

- Your chakras are not just little energy fields that spin in your body to connect your organs to your body energetically. They are far more. They are your protectors, they communicate with each other, they communicate with everything around you, they constantly connect to everyone you know. When you are walking down the street they are checking if you are safe. When you are alone, they are your awareness that tells you if someone has come close. When the phone rings and you know who it is even before you answer, it is your chakras that are recognising that person's energy before they call.

- The chakra energy released from the front of the body relates to the past, and the chakra energy released from the back of the body relates to future. You know your past and can see it, so it is the front of your body, you cannot see your future, so it relates to back of the body.

- Our chakras have a centre point which connects to our body from our soul and then vents, vibrating from the soul through the body and out towards the world communicating with your surroundings. The chakras vent energy out from the front and back and side vents.
- The base chakra vents down into the legs and connects to hips.
- The sacral chakra vents into the groin area and ovaries.
- The solar plexus chakra vents out the side towards the elbows.
- The heart chakra vents out towards the sides and the upper arms (relating to lymph nodes under the arms).
- The Throat chakra has large side vents in the neck.
- The Third eye vents out the temples and its rear vent is on the cranial line just below the skull.
- The crown chakra vents directly into the lobes of the brain.
- They are all connecting with each other and to important parts of your body so that you can be aware and safe in your life.
- A chakra can be out of position in the body and with conscious awareness it can be moved back into its centre.
- Your chakras can be damaged and when cleaned and repaired with healing will recreate themselves instantly.

- Trauma in the chakras can physically affect the body parts relating to that chakra. They affect these areas because they are energetically a part of the area.
- Your diaphragm is a part of your solar plexus chakra and your heart is a part of your heart chakra.
- It is possible to clean and clear your own chakras with love and acceptance.
- The base, sacral, and solar plexus chakras are our earth bound human chakras.
- The crown, third eye, and throat chakra are our universal soul chakras.
- The heart chakra is the balance and connection between your soul purpose and your human life.
- The action of a chakra can shape your body - a blocked or slow base chakra can cause weight gain over the hips and upper legs.

Base Chakra

- When you clear a base chakra it can change all the chakras considerably, so I always work on the base chakra first.
- Base chakra trauma is related to pre-life, womb and unconscious awareness energetics. It holds our unconscious patterns created when we are children under seven years of age.
- Base chakra trauma can cause a person to have overweight hips and have a pear shaped body.
- Trauma in the base chakra can affect the heart chakra.

Sacral Chakra

- Sacral holds flight and fright trauma responses.

- It can also hold freeze trauma response, which I feel is a response that causes people to get stuck in their lives, finding it difficult to let go of the past. Freeze relates to being in a situation where you can't run or fight. For example, if you are a child with bullying parents or siblings, you can't fight them because they are too big, and you can't run away because you are not old enough to look after yourself, so you just freeze, waiting and hoping for the trauma to stop.
- Sacral chakra affects peoples' wrists.
- Trauma in the Sacral can affect the throat chakra.

Solar Plexus Chakra
- Your solar plexus chakra is like a lake of emotion.
- When it is flat and calm, it is holding your emotional reactions in harmony.
- When it has a rough surface, the emotional needs of your humanity are not being met.
- Fear can be overwhelming you, or your needs are not being met even if you are screaming them.
- It is the chakra that defines your human needs outwardly into the world.
- It is the internal voice of your base and sacral chakra for you to experience what you are emoting and feeling.
- Solar Plexus chakra affects elbows.
- Trauma in the Solar Plexus chakra can also affect the Third Eye Chakra.

Heart Chakra
- The heart chakra is busy trying to balance out our souls needs compared to our human needs and is affected when you do not follow what feels right for you

and choose instead what is expected of you by parents, partners, siblings, children, friends, and society.

- A blocked heart chakra (which I believe relates to breast tissue dis-ease) relates to not being true to yourself, which is a childhood learned behaviour.
- We are taught that girls should become mothers, carers, and cooks and to put their needs aside for their children and husbands. So we teach girls to ignore their soul needs and expect them to fulfill the expectations of society.
- We tell men that they should not have emotions, that emotions are bad and nurture is for women. "Big boys don't cry!" So we disconnect our boys from their emotions, and thus they learn not to accept their emotional needs.
- The heart chakra can also be affected by ancestral and past life beliefs.
- Heart chakra blocks affect the heart, breasts, upper arms and shoulders.

Throat Chakra

- Throat chakra trauma manifests in pain or illness in the mouth, jaw, shoulders, and neck. It can relate back to trauma from being allowed to cry too long as a child. As a baby the only way we can communicate is through crying. If this is not recognised, it creates trauma in our throat chakra which is triggered in our adult lives if we are not being heard or recognised.
- It also has powerful connection to obesity, because crying as a child is related to asking for nourishment, nurture, and security. If a person has not received this recognition as a child, then the adult will eat to try and

give themselves the feeling of nurture and security. This will also be held as a trauma in the sacral chakra.
- Throat chakra affects throat, teeth, neck, shoulders and the cranial energy.

Third Eye Chakra
- This Chakra controls the left/right balance of energy in the body. This relates to balance in masculine and feminine energy, acceptance and confidence, being submissive and dominant, giving your power and holding your power.
- The third eye allows you the awareness of your place in your earth bound universal purpose, helping your creativity and reasoning to merge into skill and flow, allowing you to create an idea and to cognitively make that idea a reality.
- Being in tune with your third eye can create euphoric sensations.
- Your third eye can affect your sight and hearing.

Crown Chakra
- Crown chakra is a universal energy portal that works in connection with your base chakra to keep your soul energetically fed and to allow life-giving energy to flow through you.
- Your crown chakra is indirectly controlled by your base chakra because it can only flow as much energy into your body as what is being grounded out of your body.

Over Active Chakras
- This type of person usually owns the trauma that has created the chakra to change its energetics. They have

accepted their outcome and believe they are not worthy or wrong and thus give the chakra the power to stay the same. They are afraid of change as well as have no idea what change is needed.

• People with over-active chakras tend to be skinny and anxious with their energy flowing very fast as they live their lives.

Under Active Chakras

• This type of person usually knows deep down that it is not their fault, but will hold a trauma to keep themselves safe. They are living a life according to other peoples' external beliefs that they know deep inside are not true for them, but they are not certain how to let these go and change their world. They are afraid of change.

• People with under-active chakra tend to be overweight and bubbly, their energy is very outward as a protection, and find it difficult to be entirely genuine.

In sharing this information, I think it becomes apparent how important learning about your own chakras is for your own good and for that of your clients. So learn to be open in your chakra energy when you are working with a client, and with practice, it will become automatic. Doing the Five Breath Exercises will be a trigger to opening your chakras as you progress with your own development. However, there are lots of different methods of learning how to open and close your chakras through meditation, mindfulness, and movement. I suggest you find the way that suits you and practice it!

Your chakras are extremely important in your life right now, every moment, all the time. When was the last time you spent time actively, consciously connected to your own energy?

CHAPTER FIVE - THE POWER OF TOUCH

So many of us go through our lives with way too little physical connection. Touching is so important as a healer and of great benefit to so many clients, so we must be comfortable with it and be aware that our touch is coming from the correct intention that has the intention of well-being and comfort.

I remember my first paying client's session as if it were yesterday. He contacted me out of the blue. I do not recall how he came to hear about me. He lay down on my healing couch. I sat in my chair next to him and I stared at him. I was supposed to be putting my hands on him to give him healing but I was afraid, afraid to place my hands on his body! I remember having to remind myself that this man was paying me to put my healing hands on him. All my focus was on the fact that my hands were touching his clothing and pressing on his body and I was still afraid I might get into trouble. I remember that I couldn't even imagine giving him a whole hour of healing which felt like a very long time. At the end of the healing session, he sat up and told me that he had had many healing sessions from many different people and that he had never experienced anything that strong before. That the way I connected to him made he feel relaxed and calm. I smiled with a fake knowingness that I had done well. In reality, I was blown away! I didn't know that I was powerful, I didn't know I was good at this, I was just doing it because It was what I had to do. I also realised that that first client had been in great need of connection and touch.

There are several clients for whom I give part of the session over to focusing on nurture and tenderness. I may stroke their hair very slightly, move my hand along their shoulder more than normal, and stroke energy down their legs or arms, making sure my touch is reassuring, attentive, and has the intention of well-being and I also have very clear protocols that I simply do not break.

When my guides wanted me to put my hand directly onto a client's base chakra, I refused! So they showed me that there is a very strong connection into the base chakra through the hip joint! So with the base chakra, I always work directly through the hip joint usually on the left of the body. If I need to work on the sacral chakra or gut and hip issues, I will put my hand very close to sensitive areas, but to do this, I inform my clients first and allow them to show me what is appropriate for them, even if it means not working with touch.

When I had a client with breast cancer, she gave me permission to touch her breasts. She told me that every doctor and nurse she had seen over months had fiddled with her nipples, and it did not bother her. Nevertheless, because I don't ever need to put my hands where it is not appropriate, I worked from a few inches away, which is not a problem - I can also work thousands of miles away

Different Hand Movements

To develop our skills, we must allow our intuition to help us, and I want you to learn that it is ok for you to do what feels right. With this in mind, rather than just using 'normal' hand positions, I use many different hand movements to connect to my clients. Please be aware that these techniques are extremely gentle and need to be used with the utmost care and respect for the client's body. I always ask a client for permission first and continue to check in with them all the way through the work to make sure they are happy to continue. As healers offering intuitive hands on healing, we are not supposed to be adjusting or manipulating peoples bones or muscles. To do that you would need further training and certification but that does not mean that we cannot energetically suggest to the body that it should shift into its normal state of being

1 - Tapping

I will tap and tap on a client's body, sometimes thousands of taps in a session. Even when I am working with a client over Skype, I will find myself tapping my work table knowing that I am triggering release in the client even though they are far away.

- Tapping connects through the skin, tissue, muscle, and fascia, vibrating deeply down into the bone and can clear energy held in the skeleton.
- Tapping also works on helping the meridians to become more aware; think of it like plumbing with you banging on the pipes to see which is blocked or not!
- When you tap, you are sending vibrations down the meridian lines of the body creating awareness and a wave of energy that will shift stagnant energy and trigger the body and soul into investigating that flow of energy, which creates awareness and this awareness, creates change for that energy line.

• A tap on a random spot on a client's body can also bring their minds into the moment and distract them from blocking the healing.

2 – Pressing

Pressing on a spot you are intuitively drawn to on a client's body is a wonderful way of releasing trauma and pain from the body, so do not be afraid to push on those spots. It is called acupressure and is a form of acupuncture. It is a wonderful experience to be pushing on a joint or muscle and actually feel the energy shift in that spot - I usually feel as if the entire client, room, and energy have shifted - and I am in a new place.

• You can use a finger, thumb or hand to push on a spot. Choosing which is mainly common sense. I mostly use fingers but will use my hand on a client's buttock muscle, or very gently on their shoulder to create a release. I may push quite hard on the buttock muscle, but be very gentle on the shoulder.

• Be aware that to some clients the lightest touch can be painful, and very often we push on a spot that we are drawn to, that the client doesn't even know is holding pain. This is very relevant for the cartilage and fascia around the ribs and joints in the body.

• If I have a client who is very sensitive to touch and cannot handle my pushing or even touching that area, I cup my hand around the spot so that the very light pressure of my hand is around the tender area and my hand chakra is directly over it. With my other hand, I push on the identical spot on my body. Amazingly, I have often found that there is tenderness in my body in that same place.

- Pressing on the face, jaw, and temples can be a wonderful place to find releases for clients - especially those with infant trauma from under 18 months old.
- If you are not sure if you are pressing too hard, ask your client. Some clients feel relief from the pain, but others may shy away from pain and cannot cope with it, so it is your job as the healer to assess what is best – with their help.

3 - Firm Short Strokes

Sometimes a spot that you are drawn to just needs recognition to help it shift. Sometimes laying on hands, or pressing works. However, firm short strokes can create a wave in the energy you are channelling, which can make a huge difference to just laying on your hands and expecting everything to happen on its own! I like to turn my hand from palm down as I stroke then up to the direction I want the energy to clear - pushing the energy to move through the body. The movements can be quick and direct.

4 - Long Strokes

Long fluid strokes down the body can be appropriate with a client whose energy seems to want to flow but has lost its natural concept of direction or movement. I find this often occurs when the body is unable to ground itself. So I use flowing strokes to ground the base chakra energy and encourage the flow to begin:

- Down the arms from shoulder to finger tips.
- From shoulder down the side of the abdomen to the hip and even down to the toes.
- From the hip joints down the legs (the most common long stroke I use!).

• Down the client's back to help increase the movement of blocks and fears for future events (remember the back of the body relates to the future).

• To clean and heal the auric field I often use long strokes which can be free flowing and natural - allowing my body to just flow with the energy of the aura - allowing my hand chakra to be open and flowing to allow the energy to be like the finest sandpaper smoothing the aura to perfection.

5 - Pulling

One of the very first techniques my guides taught me. Pulling on the fingers, pulling gently on the arm and pulling lightly on the legs. When I say pulling, it's more like a firm stroke away from the body - not a joint popping pull, but a firm caress to suggest energetic movement!

• Pulling the fingers is a wonderful way to start a healing session. We use our fingers almost every moment of the day: we tap with anxiety, we wriggle our fingers in excitement, and we point them for a multitude of reasons. We don't realise, however, that our hands hold a vast quantity of chakras and meridian flows.

• Pulling gently on the arms can trigger releases in the wrists, elbows, and shoulder, and can help release heart chakra energy by triggering a release of the muscles under the arms around the side vents of the heart.

• Pulling gently on the legs by holding firmly underneath the ankle helps release the pressure on the hip joints and knees and ankles, and helps release the heel bone. But remember, this is not a chiropractic bone adjustment. It is a firm but gentle release. The pull is designed to allow the body to become aware of its own functional situation so be very responsible when pulling.

• I will often find myself with my hands under a client's head with my fingers laying on the edge of the skull on the cranial points. This is a powerful area and must be treated with the utmost respect and worked on energetically only. I do very little pulling or pressing in this area, and if I do, it is usually softer, slower, and with more care, than any other pulls I would try.

Pulls can be from 2 seconds to 3-4 minutes. Always ask permission before you pull and keep checking in with your client that they are not in more pain or discomfort from the pull.

Use your intuition. As long as it feels right and does not offend or hurt your client, then you can try it gently.

I have students who are dancing around people's auric fields because it feels right. The resulting pulls on the auric energy creates releases that are easily felt, and work well for their clients. Trust yourself.

6 - Twists and Rolls

Quite often I find that a client's body is out of alignment with its own energy flow and is unable to communicate correctly through a joint. To enable the energy to line up I give that point a slight, very gentle twist or roll.

I mainly use this on the legs - high up by the hip - and on the shoulders. With my hands on the client's upper leg, I twist the leg very gently back and forth, causing the hip joint to rotate a small amount. It is a slow, rocking twisting motion that's just allowing the hip bone to connect to the joint and align the energy flow. It is so enjoyable when it comes into alignment! You can feel the release like a dam breaking its walls and flowing naturally once again. I have done it while demonstrating in front of 50 people, and everyone in the room became aware of the releases when I made the connection!

I have also done releases on the arms and neck by very slightly straightening the head or arm to allow the energy to align for that short moment and remind the body of its natural alignment.

CHAPTER SIX – LET INSPIRATION MOVE YOU

Whilst in the healing process you need to be aware of your physical self and allow inspiration and intuition to guide you. It is important to allow your intuition to lead you on a physical level to allow your guides to influence your body movements.

If your inspiration is to stand up and move to the other side of the healing bed, then stand up and move. Don't let what you think you are supposed to do stop you from being your own true healer. There are no boundaries to what you can do, as long as you are not offending your clients and working for their highest of good.

Here are some examples to help you understand how allowing yourself to be free with your physical intuition can help in your work.

1 – "Pull His Toes"

I was working with a middle-aged client, aware that I needed to balance his energy due to the shock to his body caused by the sudden loss of his mother. He had had to organise her funeral and look after his younger siblings in their grief. It was not until months later that he finally had time to come and see me. It had been a tough time for him, and I was aware of the energy of grief and feelings of over-whelmed responsibility trying to release from his body. To aid the release, I was working on his shoulders, focusing the healing down his body. After about 40 minutes, my intui-tion suggested that I should pull on his big toes. I got up sat at his feet and gently started to pull his big toes and in-stantly felt the energy release. Subconsciously, he had been holding onto the trauma, afraid to let go, afraid of his feel-ings, afraid to stop and mourn. The action of pulling his toes gave the energy direction and distracted his brain enough for the energy to shift and move. Then he cried. He sobbed more than any client I have had before or since. I had to wipe the healing couch dry after his session.

2 – "Turn 90 Degrees"

I had been trying to help a regular client trust herself. To get more connected on a feminine level, and to connect to her primal self. When she climbed onto the healing couch in one of her sessions, I found myself instinctively getting up and turning the healing couch 90 degrees from its normal position. In all the years I have been working with clients in my healing room I had never done such a thing. My couch was always parallel to the big window in my room. While the session didn't feel that different to me other than being in a different position, the outcome was incredible. She told me that her entire world had shifted as if she had turned a new corner. Shortly after the session, she had felt her primal female power open up and flow. Her menstrual cycle stabi-lised (after an irregular 18 months) and her business began to flourish. Physically turning the couch on which my client lay had helped her turn a corner in her life. Because I had trusted my intuition, I had been able to help her to turn that she desperately needed corner.

3 – "Clap Loud!"

A new client had come to me to deal with his inexplicable anger. After going through all my preliminary questions and initial healing, he lay down on the couch. As I was about to start hands on healing, I received a clear, intuitive suggestion to go and stand in the corner of the room as far away from him as possible. I told the client that I wasn't sure why but that it was best for me to be standing in that corner rather than starting the hands on healing for the moment. Everything was quiet. A few minutes went by until I became aware of an intuitive suggestion to clap loudly! I clapped. The client reared up and started to grunt and growl, his chest rearing up as his body went into torsion. After that, I was able to work on clearing the lost souls that had attached to him, as well as teaching him what to do to prevent holding them. By standing in that corner, I had avoided getting grabbed or struck as the entities that were trying to control him had reared up in fear.

The most common intuitive information we receive is knowing where to place our hands on a client's body without thinking about it. And we simply go ahead and trust. All I ask is that you also trust the weird stuff! Trust yourself, your guides, your intuition, and inspiration. Trust it more than you trust your clients or your teachers. Trust you and your feelings first and foremost.

4 – Weird Is the New Normal

It is important to embrace working outside the box. If you are only going to follow what you read, or have learned from teachers, without thinking outside that box - without listening to your weirdest thoughts - you are not going to develop your unique healing ability. You can learn from what I have to impart in this book, but you can never be me, and never understand everything that I am. You must feel free enough to be open to your intuition, your guides, and your inspiration. It is also important to know that you do not have to understand everything you pick up intuitively. You just have to trust yourself, making sure that you do not offend or hurt anyone in the process.

PART TWO
MENTAL HEALING

Chapter Seven - The Mental Aspect of Intuitive Healing

1 - What is Your Responsibility Toward You and Your Clients?

As healers, we must be aware of our responsibilities as an intuitive healer. We must be clear about honouring and respecting our clients. However, we must be mindful of honouring and respecting ourselves first. If we do not honour and respect ourselves, we have nothing to give our clients. Self-doubt and self-belittlement are dis-respecting yourself and your clients. Undervaluing your worthiness is dis-respecting yourself and your clients. Under-estimating the value of your time is dis-respecting yourself and your clients.

We must believe in ourselves to be clear channels. If you are having negative or belittling thoughts either consciously or subconsciously about your healing practice, then your personal issues are hindering the flow of loving universal energy from pouring through you with its clean, powerful love. Self-doubt blocks your natural flow as a healer and a person.

So how do we work without allowing doubts to hinder us?

Healing is such a wide open, inexplicable, unfathomable process that we cannot be expected to understand it all. Healing is not a 'black and white' process; it's not even a 'grey' process, it is more like a 'pinky, yellowy, orangey, greeny, bluey and purpley' process, with a hint of gold and silver, and a huge jar of faith. It is also very different for each person with each client.

Learning to have faith in yourself even if you make a mistake or get something wrong, will break through any self-doubt. Happily accepting that you could be wrong is just as important as having faith. Let me explain wrong for you. There is no wrong, bad, or mistake; for me, everything is just a learning experience so I tend not to beat myself up for the difficult learning experiences, or the ones that might make me feel insecure, or unknowing. I ask you to allow yourself to acknowledge that as a person you may not get everything as perfect as you would want. Accepting yourself gently as being infallible is a powerful life lesson.

If you discover that your intuition with a client or in your own life may not have helped you or proven accurate in a given situation, you need to acknowledge it and be 100% ok with it. Being wrong is the beginning of being right, and if you cannot handle being wrong, you will never be truly 'accurate' because your fear of being wrong will get in the way of your intuition. Fear becomes a barrier that blocks your intuitive flow, but if its ok for you to be wrong, then the fear just becomes the next lesson you are about to learn. Then fear becomes the energy pushing you into learning and discovery.

This is so important for you to learn that I am going to break it down:

If a person has chosen of their own free will to come and see you for healing so that you can help them with their healing process, then there should be no doubt whatsoever that you can help them.

Do not try to work out how you can help them. There is no point in trying to quantify something over which you have no control. You cannot control the outcome of anything in life, especially someone else's healing process.

If you doubt, you most likely do not completely believe in yourself, your guides, or your intention. If that is the case, then there is a work for you to do. Good work. The work of accepting and acknowledging yourself. But it does not mean you should stop offering healing. Never stop offering healing. Healing is the teacher that will help you to find confidence and faith in yourself. If you allow yourself to be a 'healing process student', and allow yourself to heal through the lessons healing offers you, then you are on the right path. You will begin to trust yourself as a healer and become confident and secure as a human being - believing in yourself, your abilities and your purpose (even if you have no idea what your purpose is). I'm not talking about being egotistical or over-confident. We all have an ego, and without it, we'd never achieve anything but it needs to be held in check, controlled by your awareness, not by your need to be seen, to be heard, or in a need for recognition. I always say "Don't use a big E for Ego - use a little e for ego!"

We are none of us perfect. Yet in our imperfections we are perfect - if we can accept and love ourselves. Your responsibility as a healer is to recognise that. Accept yourself as perfect, even if there are parts of you that you would like to change or patterns that you would like to redesign.

Accept your client as perfect, even if they are under extreme duress, illness, trauma or loss. They are perfect as they are in that moment. They are supposed to be feeling these things because that is their reality. Your job is to acknowledge that they are perfect. That you have been asked to help them move forward from that moment of perfect-duress into a place where the duress energy is no longer needed - into a place where they have processed those traumas, illnesses, and loss with love, understanding, and nurture, so that they may leave them behind and move forward.

Your responsibility as a healer is to accept your client as perfect and to do your job to the highest standard of your capability. It is also important to understand that when the client leaves, your job is over. Their energy may still be in a process, and they may experience more extreme healing, but for now, **your work is over**.

You cannot take responsibility for your client before or after the session. If you do, you are disrespecting both your client's needs and your own needs. The client has not come to you to ask you to live their life for them. They have come because it felt right to have you help them. Respect the time you have with your client, then allow them to be responsible for their own lives, and let them go with love.

You cannot ever expect to know exactly what help or difference you are making in their lives; you must simply have faith in their wish to see you.

A client came to me on the recommendation of a friend who had seen one of my healing demonstrations. He was visiting the UK and wanted to see me urgently. He told me that he was struggling with extreme anger - mainly towards his wife and his employees.

It was a cool autumn day when this man in his early 60's drove three hours to my home, accompanied by his wife. As we talked, I discovered that his anger was directed toward the people for whom he felt responsible.

He cried deep sobs throughout the session while his wife's mouth hung wide open - in 40 years of marriage, she had never seen him cry like this. He had come for help with his anger, and we had processed the hurt that lay beneath the anger, and he needed to cry that out.

He knew for certain I had helped him process his anger, so thanked me and requested a follow-up session. He began the second session by giving me information he had neglected to tell me in the previous session. He told me that 20 years ago he had been diagnosed with cancer and had undergone extreme treatment that had worked and he was in total remission. However, the treatment had messed up his body's natural thermostat. When it was cold, he felt warm, and when it was cool he felt hot, and when it was hot he was on fire, and he had had to organise his life in such a way to deal with this problem.

He lived in a predominantly hot country, so woke very early, worked until 11 am and returned home to his air-conditioned environment to keep cool until late afternoon when he could once again cope with the cooler temperatures outside. For the past 20 years, he had only worn shorts and short-sleeved shirts. He didn't own any jackets and only wore long trousers when he had to look smart.

Then he told me that after our first session he had noticed that he had felt a bit cool on the way home and then by late that evening he was freezing. The following day he realised that the healing session had reset his body thermostat back to normal and that he was feeling temperatures in the same way as other people. He was very pleased about this – except for the number of clothes he had had to buy to keep warm in our English autumn.

You can never be sure how the healing will affect someone. Your responsibility is to do what is right in the moment without getting in the way. In return, healing will teach you and teach you and teach you.

2 - Healing Intention

Why have you become a healer? Why are you offering healing and what is your intention?

Being clear in your intention is very important. My intention is to affect as many people as I can and to do this I want to work with people who affect people. I want to work with businessmen and women who employ people, and I want to work with musicians and actors who have the potential to communicate energetically with tens of thousands of people. I also want to help people heal because I need to heal, which is also a great and very respectful intention. And the reason I am writing these books is to help you to grow so that you can become a healer who helps others and a sharer who spreads the light.

Understanding why and what you get out of being a healer and a clear awareness of your healing path will attract clients and people to you. People who are in align-ment with your energetics and purpose will be drawn to you. Like a moth to a flame, they will simply have no choice.

A client and fellow healer asked me what marketing I do to get so many clients. I explained that I hardly do any marketing. Most clients come by word of mouth and that they come because I am at one with myself as a healer. I know what my role as a healer is and I am clear with my intentions.

When I am a clear channel, clients feel safe being with me. When I have clarity, my clients are also able to find clarity within themselves.

Recently in a fortnightly healing group, one of my regular clients appeared to be uneasy. Something I hadn't seen in her since she first joined the group. I asked her what was going on for her. She said that the group is usually a place where she feels safe and free - one of the reasons she keeps coming – but today she was feeling uneasy and unsafe. I asked her why she normally felt safe in the group and she said it was because I made her feel safe - that I held a safe environment in which she did not feel judged or threatened. I asked "Why not today?" and she replied that she wasn't sure. As it happened, that morning I had had a therapy session that had helped me shift a significant childhood trauma and so was not as grounded as usual. I then fo-cused on grounding myself and the room softened. Shortly afterwards she told us that she felt safe again.

Just trying to be your true self in your true intention, even if you are not yet 100% sure of your intention, will draw people to you. Again it is simply self-acceptance.

3 – Clarifying your Intention

Following are some important questions for you to consider. Questions I ask myself over and over as I grow as a healer. It has taken me years to get to the point of being aware enough to be 100% genuine in my answers, so don't worry if you cannot answer them all straight away. Yet it is necessary for you to look deep within to find what the true answers are for you in this work.

Why do I want to offer healing?

Have you worked out why you are drawn to offering healing?

- For financial reasons?
- Because you need healing?
- Because you are a rescuer?
- Other reasons ....

What do I get out of it?

How do you feel after a healing session?

- Do you get a fix of pride, or do you feel full of doubt?
- Do you feel that you have done what you needed to do to earn a living?
- Other reasons ....

Where is my ego in the healing progress?

Are you enjoying being the healer and helping people?

- Does it make you feel special?
- Do you feel at one, calm and pleased to be of service?
- Other reasons ....

Am I genuine to myself as a healer?

- Do you actually enjoy the process of being a healer?

- Are you in charge of being the healer, or is the healer in charge of you?
- Other reasons ....

Am I allowing the healing sessions to heal me too?
- Is this process of being a healer helping you to grow in yourself and in your healing ability?
- Are you being healed through your work?

Am I clear with my beliefs in exchange for healing?
- Are you valuing your healing?
- Are you worthy of exchange of your time and ability?
- Are you comfortable with what you earn or receive in return for your help?

Are you allowing yourself to be the intuitive healer you truly are?
- Are you trusting your intuition as a healer?
- Do you let your brain get in the way - not trusting your intuition because you are blocking being true to your ability?

I believe it is important to discover the answers to these questions to be the best channel and healer you can be, but I'd like to make it very clear that there are no wrong answers, this is about self-discovery and self-enlightenment, not a way of wronging yourself.
- If your true purpose is to offer genuine healing because it is who you are, that is brilliant.
- If the financial reward is the biggest draw, you will attract people who have the same or directly opposite beliefs to you.

- If you are a healer because your childhood behavioural pattern is to rescue people, then you will draw people who need rescuing because you have the understanding and skills to work with them.

As you continue learning about yourself, you will find you draw different clients because of the changes in yourself and your intentions.

Over the years I have found that I attracted clients who needed to find their way and those who were in the process of defining themselves. Then suddenly I had clients who knew who they were and needed help with courage to move forward. Then clients who were on the brink of success. And then there were clients who were successful but didn't realise it. These clients were mirrors for me to heal myself. I helped them heal, and in return, they helped me to heal.

Whatever clients you attract, you will help them grow and change if they need to change and the same will happen to you. And if you find it difficult to accept and understand them and find yourself ridiculing or judging your clients, then you will have the opportunity to heal those traits within yourself.

4 – Intention of Exchange

When it comes to being a positive, powerful healer whose clients find you because your intentions are clear and genuine, the business part of you - the intention of exchange - must also be thoroughly acknowledged. What are your financial intentions as a healer?

This is a fundamental question to ask and is an issue that needs to be clarified because it can affect the flow of energy you channel. If you are healing without being at one with your financial intention, monetary concerns can weave their way into a session. Feelings of not being fully valued or worries about a bill which can't be paid can interrupt focus and occupy space you should be using for your client.

Financial worries are a powerful deterrent to being at one with yourself, so creating a clear understanding of how finances work is essential. I am not a trained businessman. I have no business advice to offer other than to repeat that you need to be clear on your financial intention. I can only offer a breakdown of my own beliefs and you can feel if they are correct for you or not.

To be of help to my clients, I need to be in as calm a space in my life as possible. Knowing that I can pay my bills and taxes makes me feel better about myself, which means I can be a far better channel. My clients want me to help them with their healing process because I have the skills that they need. The session takes up my personal time, which I am willing to offer, but needs to be reimbursed because this is my career and I need to pay my way in life. There must be an exchange that makes both client and healer feel that we have both benefitted from the transaction.

Early on in my career, I clarified my financial intention. I believed that there must be an exchange, because if I offered healing to clients without charging for my time or insisting on a clear exchange, then the clients were not going to put value on the healing process and diminish the potency of the healing.

In the beginning, I charged for my time, but not for the healing. I gave up my time to be present and available for the process, but the healing was free because I was learning from the healing and I was simply the channel. These days I charge for my time and also for the unique set of skills and understanding that has taken many years to acquire.

Because I use money to purchase the things I need, and things that cannot be 'exchanged' in our day and age, I prefer to be reimbursed financially. I have not yet had a client who wants to exchange car insurance for a healing session! To obtain the things I need to survive in this world, I work in the common currency; cash money.

Aware that I need to value my time correctly, I take into consideration that I should try not to see more than 20 hours of clients a week. More than that and I am messing with my level of tiredness, and that means I might not always be giving of my very best. If I know that I am going to see more clients than the optimum 20, I have to put in a few days of total rest. I also take into consideration that I can-not guarantee a constant flow of clients. They ebb and flow as they should, or I would not be doing my job correctly. Breaking down what I need to earn each week to take care of my expenses, and dividing that by an average of 12 cli-ents a week is my way of finding an appropriate fee to charge.

Having my financial intention in place helps me to un-derstand why I charge the amount I charge. It helps me feel comfortable accepting the financial exchange I believe I deserve. This gives me confidence in myself and helps me realise my worth to my clients. Since my clients keep re-turning and recommending me to their friends and family, I know my intention is in the right place and that I am deal-ing with it genuinely. Healing is my profession, and as a professional healer, I need to feel the benefit, and financial reward is one of the many ways that happens.

If you feel that you are not charging enough, then you are not charging enough.

If a client cannot afford to see you and they ask for a reduced rate and you agree, it is important to recognise that it was your choice and that you are responsible for the earnings of that session. I do accept clients at a reduced rate if they are courageous enough to ask, but only after listening to my intuition.

I received a call from a lady who had seen me demonstrate 12 years before. She said she just wanted to chat about healing and I was happy to give her 5 minutes of my time. She went on about her dire situation and talked about the fact that although the National Health System was free it did not give her the opportunity to see healers like me. At this point, I started to be suspicious about her intentions. She ended the call by asking if I was still seeing clients in her area and asked how much I charged for sessions.

The following day I got a text message from her asking for a session. I texted back offering some appointments. She then texted that she couldn't afford the session and could I offer a discount. My intuition stepped in saying NO, NO, NO, which I acknowledged, but I was interested in seeing how the interaction would play out.

I texted asking her what she could afford. She answered with an amount that was less than 10% of my normal hourly rate. After room hire, travel costs and expenses, I would have been paying for a good part of her session. I became aware of my lesson in all of this. She was asking me to take responsibility for her healing process.

To communicate directly and make it clear where I stood, I called her. I explained that my expenses cost £15 more than she was willing to offer, which meant that I would be paying for her healing and that she was asking me to take responsibility for her healing which I was not willing to do. Instead, I offered her a 20-minute phone healing session at the rate she had offered. I explained that as a healer I want to help people, but I can't help them if I am not happy and clear with the process so I would be very happy to help her long distance. She was very pleased, and we booked a session for a few days later. The day before the session, she cancelled, and I have not heard from her since.

I am in great appreciation of the lesson I learned. She wanted me to take responsibility for her, and I believe that had I offered the original session at my expense, she would have wanted more and more and more.

To have a clear mental process and a clean healing experience for my clients, my intention is to have a clear transaction with my client where we both end up with a feeling of worth from the session.

5 - Observation

It is important to practice an awareness of your mental self during a healing session, to observe yourself, your surroundings and your intuition while you are healing. I am observing myself and observing my client throughout the healing session which assists me to accept any external stimuli. For instance: unusual movements in the healing room, my personal spirit connection, my physical responses and my client's physical emotional and mental reactions while I am working with them. I might observe that I felt a heavy feeling about something a client has just said, and I am aware of its importance although I may not as yet know why it is important.

I was working in another country when a 25-year-old woman who didn't speak good English came to see me and brought her boyfriend as translator. She was suffering from severe anxiety. The doctors had offered her medication but she didn't want to take it. She gave me all her childhood background, but nothing particular stood out for me. As she lay on the healing bed, I felt into her anxiety. I was just sitting connected to her body, observing myself observing her. There was a slight feeling of a shift in her energy, and intuitively I followed it. It gave off an energetic pulse that I observed, but my observing mind that was observing me noticed that that energy pulse reminded me of another client with a similar energy pulse and it triggered an idea in my head. I asked, "Have you every used recreational drugs?" Her boyfriend gasped in surprise and said: "We were embarrassed to tell you that her anxiety started the day after she used recreational drugs for the first time." Now I had a place from which to work. My observing mind had helped me both find a door into helping her, as well as helping the client and her boyfriend feel confident in me and my healing process.

In the process of observing my client, I am also observing myself as the healer in the process of offering healing. This process of observing yourself in the healing flow gives you the ability to learn more about your clients and at the same time learn more about healing, and how you work within your healing process.

6 - What Should You Be Thinking While Healing?

Before I began healing I had never spent an entire hour letting my mind be quiet. None of my family or friends had ever meditated or even talked about meditation, and I had no inkling of what it meant to 'connect' or 'observe' myself internally. It was to be a steep and daunting learning curve for me - as it might be for you.

Thinking stops you from being strongly grounded and slows down the healing energy flow available.

So what you are thinking is very important whilst you are working with a client. I work hard to make sure I am in observation with my clients. I am observing what is going on for them, and me, and I wait. Waiting is a key part of being quiet in your mind; I try not to get too involved with what I think my client's needs are right now. I am not afraid to say nothing, do nothing, and wait for as long as it takes for me to observe the intuition coming into my awareness. I always have a clock in view and in some of my workspaces I have 2 or 3 clocks so I can see them from different angles. The clocks are there so that I feel comfortable with what time it is and how long I have been waiting. Sometimes it's seconds, sometimes it is many minutes before I get something to follow, or intuition brings me what I need to focus on. I am not in a hurry. I have learned that keeping my mind clear of random thoughts speeds up the process of intuition. The more you practice observing your waiting, the quicker intuition comes in and then again, sometimes it is there before you even begin the healing:

Just yesterday I had a 12-year-old client with a muscle twitch that was embarrassing to her. Her doctors had told her that it would eventually go away. As she sat down for our session I had a knowing that this young lady was putting so much pressure on herself to do well in school and prove herself worthy, that she was holding a good deal of fear and worry in her body. I could feel it, see it and relate to where and how it was triggering her. The amount of intuitive information that was coming through had her and her mother in tears as we released and cleared her body. When she climbed off the healing couch she felt so elated, light-headed and clear, she literally staggered toward a chair. My intuition also gave me an emotional exercise to help her learn to process her stuck emotions.

7 - What Are Your Projections And Judgments On Your Client?

You have a new client booked and when you open the door you find an elderly, balding, grey haired man whose appearance is that of a dirty homeless person, with body odour that hits you like a wave of sewage, and the feeling you get from him makes you feel sick to your stomach and causes your skin to crawl.

The first thing he tells you is that he has stage 4 cancer and the doctors have told him that he has only weeks left to live.

Visualise that scenario in your mind. What would you be thinking? What is being triggered as you think about working with him? About having to sit close to that awful smell; to touch his dirty body; to connect to the sickly, almost desperate energy he is projecting; and having to hold a space within that energy.

Check your thoughts. What is your mind saying about how you can help this person whose doctors have told him that he has only weeks to live? Recognise what process your mind is going through and what thoughts could be blocking the flow of healing you could offer this client who has chosen you to help him heal.

Do you believe he is doomed because the doctors said he is? Are you wondering what on earth you can possibly do?

Can you work with that smell? Can you control the sickness to your stomach? Can you bear to lay your hands on his dirty, sweaty clothes that probably haven't been washed in weeks? Can you get past all this, accept him as he is and centre yourself? Can you hear through his fear of death to his deepest body's needs, beyond your reactions and responses? Can you be the healer beyond your projections, judgments and personal beliefs?

Do you feel sympathy for him and feel a need to fix him? Do you think he needs sympathy, or rather does he need connection and love? Will sympathy help him, or will acceptance help him? Will sympathy just be what he is getting from every other person who knows his story and does he need that from you? What does he need from you right now?

This is a true story about a client of mine who came to my door in exactly the way I have described, and it took me a good few minutes to work through my stuff and see that this man was fighting for his life. To see that his focus was on life, not on bathing. That his need to wash his clothing came second to his desperation to beat his illness and live. That much of the smell was derived from the number of herbal remedies he had been using. That my sick feeling came from the fear and sadness that he was carrying around.

It turned out that he was not a bum, but a well-off writer trying anything that felt right to save his life.

This exercise is not about him; it's about how I felt in those first few moments of his session. I had automatically projected onto him that he was at death's door, that he was a homeless person, that he felt bad, and that he was a smelly old man. And I could not believe my judgment had been so negative and fear-based. It shocked me to the core.

It took the first few minutes of the session to recognise this in myself and release my need to judge but I did not reprimand myself. It was my first session with someone in this state, and I had never experienced a situation like this before and the lessons were huge, but they had only just begun.

I sat with him and acknowledged his illness. I acknowledged my issues within this situation and accepted that I had them - and after I did that his smell didn't bother me. And shortly after that I realised that if my hands got dirty from his clothes I could wash them. I had found my healing zone.

I then remembered a story I had read in a magazine about a man who was diagnosed with cancer and given weeks to live. Twelve years later he was still out there living his dream without having taken a single medication. He had simply given up his life to death, stopped what he was currently doing, and gone after what he loved in life. Then that reminded me of a friend who after being told she had cancer went off with some friends to America for two weeks to do some shamanic work with Native American Indians and came back cancer free.

I stopped letting his physical-self trigger me, moved back into the healer energy in which I am so comfortable, and became his helper rather than his judge. Over the next few months his sessions always ended abruptly at about 40 minutes. I believe it was because he was having other forms of healing and my helpers didn't want to overload him. And by the time he stopped coming to see me he had drastically outlived the doctor's predictions. Many clients come and go without my knowing the ultimate outcome, but what I do know is that I have done my part as well as I can for the highest of good with total integrity and beyond my understanding.

Afterwards, I spent time working on what had happened to me and I realised that when that man came to the door, I had projected onto him. When I say project, I mean I shoved my fearful judgements forcefully down his throat! That he would die, that he was old, that he was smelly, that he was disgusting, and that he was wrong. What must such a powerful negative belief feel like to the person onto whom you are projecting? Even as I write, I feel ashamed that I had to learn this lesson in such a harsh way with such an amazingly strong man. But I am also pleased to be able to share it with you to help you become aware of how projections can force negative judgements onto other people.

So from that story, you can see how your projections and reactions within yourself in connection with your clients can affect the healing process. Being aware of your projections towards your client, as well as your client's projections and beliefs projected onto you, gives you a tremendous awareness of how to be a better healer and offer more healing. The ability to accept your own projections and learn from them lifts your healing ability a great deal.

An awareness that I must also relay to you is that feeling sorry for, or feeling enormous sympathy for a client can also be a hindrance to the healing process. Empathy is lovely and important, but it is not helpful if it turns into 'rescue' energy. You can never rescue anyone. As a healer, we offer help, not rescue. If a client is projecting rescue onto you, be very aware that that is not your responsibility.

8 - The Power of Projections

It is normal for all human beings to project their energetics onto people they may feel affection for, are afraid of, or needy toward. As babies we connect to our mothers, fathers and siblings for our survival and safety and before we can do so physically or orally, we do it energetically.

We should grow out of the needy side of these energetic projections during our teenage years, but only if we have been taught to be emotionally secure when we are young. Unfortunately, emotionally secure children are far too rare in our world, and so we find ourselves energetically blaming and judging people, especially those with whom we have a strong connection.

It is primal for our parents to protect us without fail until we can protect ourselves. Likewise, we possess a strong knowing that no matter what, our loved ones will not desert us. While it is astonishing that we hurt the ones we love the most because we feel safe in playing out our traumas and blame with the people we love the most.

And we keep projecting and blaming until we own our own emotional space.

As healers, we need to be aware that clients often project their hurts onto us so we need to be observant enough not to fall into their projections and end up playing out a role in their drama.

A client came to see me about her marriage. She told me that she loved her husband dearly, but that he had a habit that was making her feel unhappy and unsafe. Every time he walked past her he would either pat her on the bottom, poke her in the breast, or make a crude sexual comment. She had spoken to him about it many times, and he responded that he was confused by his own actions, that he couldn't work it out himself and that he had never behaved like this in any other relationship. She also told me that he didn't know she had come to see me and that he would frown on someone like me, as he was extremely sceptical and religious.

I asked her if there was a reason 'she' would project onto her husband that it was ok to treat her like this? I asked if there was anything that had happened in her childhood where someone would take advantage of her physically and invade her space? She was quiet for a short while, then took a deep breath and said "I thought I had dealt with all that. When I was a child, I had had my physical space invaded by an older cousin".

I told her that it is very common for an energetic pattern that was learned in childhood to become stronger as we get older. I explained that people whose personal physical space was invaded as a child often find themselves having their personal physical space being invaded similarly in their adulthood. I explained that because of her trauma, part of her believed that it was normal for her space to be invaded, as well as not feeling sexually safe; and that she was energetically projecting this to the world around her. Her underlying fear was sending an energetic signal to her husband to fill that fear.

The normal energetics of a relationship cause people to attempt to fill their partner's beliefs because they are in a love bond. On a universal learning scale, her partner was creating the situation so that she could see it. He was creating a space for her to heal this part of herself. He was showing her herself.

We worked on her beliefs through hands-on healing. We worked energetically on releasing the negative beliefs around her childhood invasion. We also used mind-full acknowledgments. I also made her aware of her negative protection pattern so that her energy, body, and mind were all part of the process of releasing her fear of her space being invaded.

She returned the following week and told me that the day after our session, she and her husband had been cooking dinner together and even though he had walked passed her several times, he hadn't reached out to grab her. At one point, he said he felt that something was different. He seemed to be aware that the difference was in him – not feeling the need to grab at her anymore, and for the first time recognised what he had been doing and apologised.

He had fallen prey to her projections. Because he loved her, his love connection had made him fall into her projection around men and sexual safety; also because of his need to please his partner and his need to be needed.

Until we are mature enough to be aware that everything that happens to us is 100% our responsibility we don't stop projecting onto other people. The journey to 100% acceptance of our projections is a long one fraught with many lessons that I suggest we take with gentleness and self-patience. It is tough to grasp that we are totally responsible for everything in our lives and that everything that has happened to us and is happening for us in our world right now is our creation and thus we must be responsible for it. Even if we are not to blame for what happened to us in the past, we need to take responsibility for how we are dealing with it 'now'.

If we are holding onto events with feelings of guilt, shame, anger, jealousy, envy or sadness, we are generating the perfect atmosphere to create pain and dis-ease, which can only weigh us down and inhibit our growth. Being brave enough to roll with the punches that our reality holds, by learning the lessons and forgiving ourselves allows us to move forward in a way that is energetically smooth and flowing.

It is always easier to 'blame and remain'. We blame other people for our feelings caused by the energetic trauma energy held in our bodies, thus remaining in the same pattern 'again'. We may not like the idea of taking responsibility for our trauma because we are afraid of the emotional response that it creates in our bodies. The response makes us feel far too vulnerable and may leave us with feelings that there is something wrong with us.

Most of us haven't been taught the tools we need to deal with our emotions when they explode powerfully through us stripping away our emotional barriers and protection. Lessons are much easier to carry than traumas, so once we acknowledge that 'traumas' are 'lessons', it is much easier to let go of them and the emotional energy that we have been carrying around for years.

I always say: **"being in it - is binning it"** and **"ignoring it - is storing it"**.

Being in your emotions releases them and makes you feel free and fresh. Ignoring them stores them in your energetic field which will eventually create dis-ease and pain.

9 - What Your Client Projects Onto You

There have been many times when I have found myself ignoring a client for a moment or two in a session, I immediately know that it is a sign that the client is projecting a belief that I have accepted and begun to fulfill. The projection might be that they don't count, are not seen, not heard, that their opinion doesn't count, that no one can meet their needs, etc. Having recognised the pattern, I reject it but write down the belief I feel is the strongest to work on with the client later. I then find my grounded centre, open up love, accept that love throughout my body, and then allow the love to flow to the client. I then listen to them, hear them, feel that they are worthy and want to hear their opinions.

By refusing to accept a client's self-belittling projections and opening love up to them, I have seen amazing reactions. Clients who have lost track of what they are saying as soon as I connect to them; clients starting to cry as the energy of love connects; I have also seen clients literally wilt energetically and let go of their need to hold stress in their muscles.

My favourite memory is of a client who simply started to giggle. She giggled and giggled for almost 40 minutes. The non-acceptance of her negative beliefs triggered her into the giggling child energetics that so needed to be heard. We had a wonderful session giggling and working on her energy, resulting in huge shifts. To this day she often reminds me of that session, telling me how much it helped her stop being so tough on herself, and that it's her favourite story when people are chatting about the subject of self-love and healing.

Projections are often the expectations of how we expect to be treated. If a client had parents that expected them to be independent – standing back and not helping them with the tools they needed to deal with their life issues, the client will project on you that you cannot help them with their issues. That is their belief, and because of this projection, you might find yourself feeling fed up with your client's attitude, or even feeling that you want to tell them off. You might even want to tell them that you don't feel you can help them and want to suggest other methods of healing!

You need to watch every reaction you are having, everything you are feeling, and thinking whilst with a client. I often sense a client's projection and what that triggers in me from the moment I connect with them - whether by email, 'phone, or even via a message. If the initial contact for a booking feels different in some way, I start taking note of what is going on for me. I don't make any concrete judgments because it is too subtle to be very accurate, but I am aware enough to sense that something may be different about the session that will affect me as well as the client. It might be that the client is nervous. It might be that their energy has similarities to my own, or one of my parents or siblings, which gently triggers something in me. More often than not the client projects a fear of being vulnerable, or unsafe, or of being seen through, and of wanting to be in control of the situation.

I usually let this information sit with me during the client's session and won't take it into account unless it reacts strongly in me again. But being aware of what happens to me in all connections with clients allows me to be aware of my projections and of the projections the clients have on me. All of which gives me an edge in being able to help them that much more.

10 - Emotional Energetics

Allowing yourself to be aware of a client's projections onto you, can provide invaluable information, and that often includes the client's emotional energetics. These are the emotional needs the client is unaware they are holding, or have not yet been able to deal with. The most common of these are anger, hurt, betrayal and fear. Holding onto these kinds of emotions for too many years can create severe disease in the body.

Just being able to gently make them aware that blocked emotions could be hurting them can trigger clients into beginning to process their unseen or ignored emotions and traumas. I often tell a client that I feel hurt and sad when I connect to a story or situation that has happened to them - even if they haven't told me about it. (explaining that as they have chosen to see me, it is my job to be aware of situations that have occurred in their life). When I feel angry with their mother, or brother in line with their anger, it creates a space for their body to receive the message that it is ok for them to deal with their emotions. I will then work on these held emotions as a priority.

Checking In

As a healer, I want to teach my clients how to deal with both their emotional trauma and their projections. I advise the use of a tool which I call 'Checking In'. It is a process which helps people become aware of what is going on with their emotions and feelings, and to feel comfortable with them. The process is simple but challenging in the beginning. I taught myself by stopping and checking in with my emotional state up to 2,000 times a week until I became aware of my emotions quickly and without fear! Here it is:

Stop

Stop what you are doing safely. If you need to walk away from a situation make an excuse to go to the toilet; ask your partner to give you some time to process; tell the kids to play on their own for 5 minutes; find somewhere safe to pull over if you are driving or operating heavy machinery.

Breathe

Close your eyes. Breathe. Really focus on your breathing for a few breaths to allow your mind to start to clear.

Check in

Check what is going on in your thinking mind. Check what you are feeling and try to recognise the emotion or emotions that you are experiencing.

Imagine you are bringing your thinking mind down into your body as you breathe.

Take a few breaths and observe what emotions you are experiencing.

How are you in yourself right now, at this moment?

Observe your emotions and cognitively allow yourself to **feel** rather than think these feelings.

Allow yourself to experience the emotional vibration or feeling, even if you do not know what it is. Experiencing it is more important than understanding it.

If you become afraid or uncertain of what you are feeling, just touch into it for a second or two.

If you suddenly want to stop and pull away, allow yourself to stop and pull away.

Acknowledge

Acknowledge what you are feeling through inner dialogue. Tell yourself "It is ok to be feeling this way, it is ok to be angry, it is ok to be sad, it's ok to be anxious, it's ok to feel fear."

Depending on what you are feeling, acknowledge and confirm the emotion to yourself. Even if you have no idea of what it is, still acknowledge it in yourself. "I can feel this; it's ok to feel this."

Understand

Try and understand why you are feeling the emotion or emotions. It is not overly important to understand them, but it can help to release them from your mind.

Be careful not to blame others for your emotions, these are your emotions, and you must take responsibility for them, even if someone else is to blame for the trauma or for triggering them. "This is what I am feeling, and I need to deal with it within myself."

The more you practice, the easier it gets.

Practice 'Checking In' with yourself. Bringing your mind into your emotions until you know the difference between your own and someone else's projections is a great tool.

If you find that you have been triggered into fulfilling a client's, partner or friend's projections, don't get upset with yourself, just recognise that you need to work on it. It's completely ok to go back to and remember that moment in your mind's memory and watch how you behaved. Replay the situation. Visualise yourself being in that memory, try and understand why you were triggered, and offer yourself and the person who triggered you, love, acceptance, and understanding. Doing this makes you a powerful healer, friend, and companion.

11 - Communication

Bringing your intuition into play helps you adjust your communication with each client. How you communicate with them has a huge impact on what they hear, absorb and take home with them.

- Be careful not to put your clients on a pedestal and treat them as if they are more important than you.
- If you come across too nice and sweet, they will take no notice of you.
- If you come across as all knowing, opinionated and forceful, you will push them away, and they will close down.
- If you come across caring, confident, aware of your beliefs and respectful of their beliefs, they will be inclined to listen and take what feels right to them.
- Don't be afraid to say the right thing even if the client might never want to see you again, but try to convey it as tactfully as possible.

Some clients just need to be heard; so be there for them, listen to them, hear them, and echo what you have heard. Just by repeating what you have heard can offer them a change in their belief structure.

Some clients need you to be all business, expecting you to do all the work on the healing couch and to speak as little as possible.

As you do more and more sessions and establish your own 'normal' communication mannerisms, and then find yourself communicating differently it could be:

- that you have fallen into your client's projections and are speaking to them in the way they expect to be spoken to
- it could be a clue to discovering an important element about their healing needs

You will also come to recognise similarities in questions and reactions in various clients.

One client came who was a talker. She told me about several different relationships, including parents, partners and friends and the effect they were having on her. As she went through a few of the stories, I noticed that the emotional energy I was receiving was exactly the same for each story. It was a familiar energy, common to many clients. After ten minutes I interrupted her and said: "So what I hear you saying is, no matter what you say, or how you say it, none of the people in your life are listening to you, that you are not being heard at all." Then I asked, "Who is actually there for you in your life?"

Her reaction was slow at first. She went quiet as her emotions reacted to the new conscious awareness she was processing and no longer able to stay in her mental mind they threatened to overwhelm her. After all the work she had done on herself, through all the awareness she had gained, she had never seen that no one was there for her and no one was actually listening to her! In that moment she felt the hurt of it. She experienced the truth of herself for herself, and although she was hurting, that hurt was also healing and flowing.

We went on to work on where the pattern had originated; worked through the energy around her realisation by connecting to the beliefs around that trauma; and worked on the healing couch for physical release.

We worked energetically and mentally through words and visualisations, focussing on what made her believe she was not worthy of being heard or seen.

And finally, we worked on how to go about getting her needs met.

Always keep in mind that you are the healer, not the rescuer. I often tell clients I cannot make choices for them, that it's up to them to make their own choices. You cannot fix the client's reality, but you can be there for them in that session. Some clients want to be led and told what to do. As healers, that is not our job. We are there to help clients on their path, not to write their path for them. I have sometimes found that this type of client can even twist words to save themselves from changing. So we must be careful in what we say and clear in our understanding of how they are interpreting it.

A client came for help in understanding what it was that 'she' was doing to create such a difficult, aggressive relationship in her marriage. At some point in the session, I explained the difference between men and women on an emotional level. I explained "In an average relationship, women are like the sea - constantly moving and changing, with ups and downs in their emotional responses. Men are like the land - they need an eruption, an earthquake or an explosion to make them change on an emotional level". I also said that I believed that "Women often try to erode the man's land, to shape them into the men they personally need. Most men don't respond positively to that, which causes heated arguments and the relationship to become rocky". I was trying to gently get through to her that holding her own power in the relationship would be far more gratifying than expecting him to change to satisfy her needs by constantly pestering or nagging at her husband.

A year later she came back to see me and told me that she had caught her husband cheating on her and that she had told him that "We are the the sea and the land and we were meant to be together." Taken aback, I reiterated what I had originally said and why!

It is, therefore, useful to ask at various stages during a session what the client has learned about themselves so far - to gauge what they have observed and understood, and what they have not.

As healers, we have nothing to gain from giving a client the answers they should be finding for themselves. We can suggest ideas and put forward opinions - as long as we allow the client the space to choose for themselves when and if they are ready. You also need to keep in mind that that does not stop a client from hearing something differently or inaccurately.

12 - Beliefs

No matter how passionate you are about your beliefs, they may not be your client's beliefs and it is not your job to force them on your client. Nor is it your job to wrong your clients for not believing what you believe. Not to say that you cannot share your beliefs with your client by saying things like "What I believe is…What I would do in that situation is to…" but you must also say to your clients "This needs to be your choice and needs to feel right for you." And since your client has chosen to see you, they will be receptive to genuine beliefs offered freely and take on what is right for them, without your needing to push anything on them.

Anyway, who is to say any of us is right. This entire book may just be a figment of my very active imagination! But one thing is for certain, if you expect someone to do what you think is right for them, then you are judging them as wrong and still have more work to do on yourself.

If you do not feel you are on the same page as a client about their circumstances, ask them what they believe and try to understand their point of view. You do not want to be just another person who doesn't understand them, hear them, or see them. Even if their point of view is obviously flawed they have a right to it, and a journey to learn their own lessons. In this type of situation if they are willing to evolve their point of view into a healthier understanding, I would carefully give them helpful, open and gentle information. At the same time realising that I am just a human being and might be incorrect in what I believe is the best to help my client to heal. If I am wrong, I would immediately apologise and try again to hear and understand without judgment.

A 26-year-old client who came to see me stated that she was not supposed to be alive because her parents had conceived her in their teens during a one-night stand. She had no connection with her father at all, even though he had lived nearby for most of her life; and her relationship with her mother was scatty and damaged at best. She explained that her self-belief and confidence was very low. That she had given her life to helping other people who were in need because "As she had no real purpose on the earth plane she might as well just give to others." She was clear that she was not supposed to have been born, but wanted me to help her to feel better about being alive so she could have a happier time with her partner.

I sat quietly for a moment before responding. I told her that I saw her situation in a very different light and asked if it would be ok to explain my point of view and she agreed.

It appeared to me that the universe urgently needed her on the earth plane and that for her to be born at the right time, in the right place, the universe had used two unaware puppets. The one-night stand had been a way of getting her here, alive on earth so that she could have the chance to fulfill her true purpose - a purpose beyond the sexual weaknesses of her parents. That the universe had chosen them because they were easily manipulated into creating her very important universal life; that it was understandable that she felt sad about her lack of parental connection, but that sometimes there are bigger things at play. Her purpose was beyond her parental needs.

As her thoughts processed this new information, they opened a shift in her energy and her face changed before my eyes.

She had only ever seen her situation from a 'poor me' perspective, which was totally understandable, but suddenly there was another point of view for her to consider. I asked her how this new perspective felt. Did it seem plausible? Her first words were "Yes. It would be very easy to manipulate my mother."

She got it. She had another story to cling onto. She suddenly realised how important her work with people in need was and how good she was at her work. She was no longer unwanted; she was no longer the product of a one-night stand. She was an essential child of the universe that was needed and had a purpose - a wonderful, amazing purpose that was so very important for her to continue.

So not falling into the same pattern or projection a client has about him or herself, is so important, as is wronging them about their beliefs. A negative viewpoint might have seen her as being totally wrong, or that she was having a pity party and should get over it. As healers, we are not here to agree with clients, nor to force our beliefs on them. We are here to use our compassion to help them grow, heal, and shift - to help them heal themselves.

13 - Compassion

Using our compassion does not mean feeling sorry for a client, or breaking down and crying - even after they have left. No, compassion is about seeing the situation from their point of view; and feeling what they feel about it from their point of view without adding your own stuff and emotions to the pot. Clients have told me stories that I dare not repeat they are so horrific. It amazes me what some people can do to others - even to their own families and children. If you allow sympathy to push out toward the client, it can belittle them further. It is important to keep the session clean by understanding what has happened to your clients with love and kindness. Feel the compassion, recognise it, but keep it to yourself. If you need to remark on a situation beware of going into "poor you" mode and try instead to say things like "That must be very hard for you, I can't imagine how hard that must have been. I can see why you feel so hurt." Hold onto your sympathy and respect your clients hurt with love and open-heartedness.

As with the earlier example, clients can take what you say the wrong way and allow your positive words to fulfil their negative beliefs, so think before you speak! Clients who have been coming to me for years have suddenly asked me to clarify something I said in their very first session and then quoted it word for word! Firstly, I couldn't possibly remember that far back, and secondly, it wouldn't be relevant anymore because they have changed.

I allow what feels right to guide what I say and do, putting my own stuff to the back of my mind. As the client has chosen to see me, I have an open door to trust myself while always making 100% certain I am working for their highest of good, not mine.

So, as a healer working for the highest good, I am always going to lead my client into the direction that feels right to me, which may not actually be in line with my personal beliefs.

Remember, everything you say to a client is relevant, so be very aware of what words and beliefs you offer them.

14 – Empowerment not Disempowerment

So many clients come to deal with their grief. Even if I could remove it, I wouldn't, because grief is a natural process, but what I can do is clear old grief energy to help them deal with the present.

A client came to me because her new relationship was going the same way as her past relationship which had been very hurtful and violent. She could see the similarities and wanted to work on why she was creating something similar.

We worked on her need to be treated this way by people she cared about and was happy when she had a realisation as to where the beliefs had originated.

She asked if I thought he would change; and if maybe he would still be right for her if she helped him. I explained that I cannot be responsible for giving her advice about staying with him or not. I also told her that I would be concerned, because in her last relationship she had held on for years in the hopes that he would change.

I suggested that she decide what was correct for her without worrying about his needs because if he were wrong for her, she would be doing both him and herself a favour by ending the relationship as soon as possible. I told her that while I could not decide for her, I could help her see all possibilities, and gave her ideas and words that would empower her, but that would not force her into a decision.

I also explained that since I was only getting one side of the story, I could not assume that I knew the truth. That I could only assist her in seeing what was happening for her right now; and help her to make the right choice in her life at that moment; even if those choices might not be what I feel or see to be right.

We must allow clients to learn their own lessons, even if it may hurt them. People need to hurt to grow, and I do not want to take a life experience away as it would not be helping them at all – it would instead be disempowering.

15 – Making Assumptions

When you think you know exactly what is going on, when it seems so obvious how to help a client– it's important not to hold on to that, as you could be totally, absolutely, wrong.

While I will go with my assessment of what I first feel from a client, I am also very open to being totally wrong. It can be very easy to get an idea and then find it is just the first step. If you become a dog with a bone, you can be so busy chewing that you might miss the rest of the skeleton. That bone may be one small part of a bigger picture. There are far too many differences in people for us to be 100% certain of anything.

A colleague who is a psychologist approached me, because he had a client with an issue that was on a more spiritual level, and he thought I would be able to help her. As I walked into the room where she was waiting I almost fell over backwards. She was one of the most strikingly beautiful women I have ever seen. I never knew it was possible to be lost for words because of someone's beauty. It took me a few moments to clear my thoughts.

We discussed her issue of never feeling that she is allowed to get what she needs and I explained how I would work on that issue and she booked a session for the following week.

When she arrived for her session, we again talked about what we were going to work on, and I explained how and why I was going to work in that way. As she lay on the healing couch and I was about to begin, I felt a totally different energy coming in. I realised there was something deeper and far more powerful underneath. I asked "Is there a belief that may be underneath all this?" and she said "Yes. I believe I am ugly".

I was blown away. I could never have assumed such a thing from a woman whose beauty had left me lost for words. I asked her why she felt this way. She told me that her two aunts, who had been much older than her mother and had been in their 60's when she was a child, had called her "their little ugly duckling" for years and it had settled into her beliefs and her body.

If I had allowed my assumption of what was to happen in that session, I would never have learned of this belief, and I would have wasted her time and money.

Never assume you are right, always look for more, look deeper, and allow the session to lead you rather than your beliefs or desires.

PART THREE
ENERGETIC HEALING

CHAPTER EIGHT – THE ENERGETIC ASPECT OF LOVE

1 – Love, Acceptance, and Acceptance of Love

I think it is important to clarify what I mean by The Energetic Aspect of Healing. I see it as the acceptance of love. The acceptance of the love within me allows me to be a clearer, stronger channel of healing so that when I am at one with the love within me, I am channelling as much energy for myself as I am for my clients.

Acceptance of love for me, as a healer, is best separated into three parts:

Love, Acceptance, and Acceptance of Love.

They exist together, and they exist apart, but we need to work towards having all three working within us for our healing and for our lives to be more in tune.

- **Love** is the ability to acknowledge that you are love and that you do love yourself.
- **Acceptance** allows you to see that all parts of your light and shadow are acceptable and normal.
- **Acceptance of Love** is the combination of accepting and loving all parts of yourself, no matter if your conscious mind is happy or not with how the different parts behave, perform, or what patterns they have.

Once you start on this path, you will find it easier and easier to be gentle, kind and loving to yourself, with a better understanding and space for personal growth.

Through the 'Acceptance of Love', you open the door to changing any part of yourself that you consciously wish to change, without the need to be negative. The aggressive or critical part of you that might be negative has already been accepted and loved and thus is more helpful and accommodating in changing or modifying our behaviours.

If you still find parts of you that are resistant to change, you need to follow that part and get an understanding of its purpose, using love and acceptance to help it become at one with your awareness. Accept the love in you for every part of yourself, and in doing this, you will allow others to connect to you with acceptance and love.

As a healer, being able to achieve this for yourself means that you can accomplish it far more productively for your clients.

The best way for me to be a great healer for myself and my clients is to work towards acknowledging total love within myself. I am not talking about ego love - "Oh! Look at my big muscles," or "I am the best healer," or "Fluff myself up" kind of love - I am talking about acceptance of every part of me as perfect as I am right now and worthy of my own love.

I believe I am made up of the Universal Energy of Love. Every molecule is made of energy. Therefore, I am 100% energy, and since I believe that energy is love, I am 100% love. It's this understanding that helps me work toward healing myself, my clients and the world. All I need to do is to learn to recognise and acknowledge the love within me. I need to work, step by step, towards recognising my love to the deepest core of my soul. Each step forward, no matter how small, increases the amount of energy I can channel and the more I can help my clients.

When I am connected to my love and am open to showing my love without fear, I become open to spiritual flow and intuition. I am in my inspiration and find it easy to connect to myself and my clients. I can be energetically standing next to a client who is physically thousands of miles away and be working on them as if they were standing right next to me. This connection to love makes me bypass the barriers time and distance humanity has created in our minds, and brings me to the centre of myself either at total oneness or as close as I can get to being in the symmetry of oneness with Universal Love.

This is a skill that I practice over and over using meditation and mindfulness. I practice it with every client I see, using my breathing awareness, and working on my mental self. As I develop this skill, I become more able to use it, and I am increasing the time I can hold the space.

I am slowly but surely becoming the love that I seek.

As a healer, being able to recreate this space of symmetry where you are an inspirational grounded intuitive, and a clear channel of love, is the most productive space you can be in to be of help to your clients. It is connecting to the genuine you.

To be able to find that space within yourself and to learn to stay in that space for as much of your time with your clients and more importantly for yourself, takes practice, practice, and practice!

You need to:

- use your physical breathing
- work on your mental clarity
- acknowledge the love within yourself
- share that wonderful connected space with your clients.

I already explained this in the section on Physical Healing, but I will reiterate that you need to practice this skill as often as you can so that you can get back to this space with ease. Incorporate it into your everyday processes – when you open the front door, the car door, just before you are about to eat a meal when you are on the toilet and so forth:

- stop
- centre yourself
- breathe
- open yourself up to the earth energy
- open yourself up to the Universal Energy and
- connect to your inner love
- check in how you are feeling, connect to your emotional state with gentle love

I was using this skill years before I understood it when I was out with friends and in night clubs! The manager of a night club I frequented told me that he had worked out that when I was in the club, there weren't any fights, and when I wasn't there it was far more aggressive.

I often demonstrate this skill to clients, groups, and students to show them how they too can develop this essential skill, and how wonderful it feels to help everyone connect. As I connect to myself slowly over a minute or two centering into myself, it leads the people with me to come closer to their own personal centre, and as I reach for and find my centre they often feel a sense of calm, a sense of connection, and a sense of acceptance.

This skill has been developing for me for a long time before I even realised it. I was learning this skill as a chef in my previous career. I used to focus on one dish at a time, let that order go and move on to the next dish. It was a way of teaching me the skill to find my centre, focus on the now, and then let it go and move onto the next order. This led to learning the ability to let go and centre myself no matter what bumps I had in life. Being able to reconnect to myself quickly and calmly no matter what has just happened for and for my clients gives me the ability to give more to my work and my life. This is why I can work on so many clients, one after another, without it tiring me. Let go, focus on the next, let go, on and on! Once I have done what I can do for my client on a loving, accepting healing level, I let them go, I let them go and heal, and I move on to help the next person who has chosen me to help them.

Yes, it takes practice, but working on yourself and your life is a big part of improving your healing skills. As you get to know and acknowledge your self-love more clearly, you are more able to be aware of your own healing zone, which will make you a far more effective healer.

2 – What Kind of Love?

As a person and a healer, I believe we must show love, compassion, and understanding to my clients. I also believe it's easy to get this mixed up at times so it is essential to learn how to hold the love as a healer in the right energy, and never cross boundaries.

So what kind of love should you, as a healer, be showing your clients?

The love of healing is non-judgmental and incorporates acceptance and safety.

You are accepting yourself and your client as perfect in the situation as it is. In your healing, loving space you feel safe being in your vulnerability and are willing to accept your faults even if you feel you have done something wrong! It is ok for you to make a mistake and it's ok for you to get hurt. If you can accept your own insecurities, then your clients will feel safe and secure in your healing space, they will not feel like they are going to be judged harshly or wronged, they become secure with you and are thus open to deep, safe healing.

You are happy to feel what your clients are feeling and to process their emotions for them. You are at peace within yourself. If you are happy to process your client's emotions, then you give them the ability to feel the acceptance of their own emotions and allow them to feel at peace with themselves.

This is the acceptance and love a healer should be showing to themselves and their clients for the purpose of healing and, hopefully, in their personal lives.

I have said over and over again all healing is self-healing, so then all love is self-love.

Love is the ability to allow connection to self first, and then to others around you, without expecting anything in return other than feeling good about that connection.

To love others is to see yourself as you truly are and thus must accept all the parts of yourself, or you are disconnected from love, and the flow of love is going to be compromised and thus compromise your healing flow.

3 – Love in the Modern World

I believe, as humans, we have fallen out of line with what love is and what love is not. We have become programmed in everyday life to believe love is the thing that happens to you when you are in a relationship; or between a parent and a child; and a child and a parent.

Love has become confused with being in-love, and lust and desire have become abused by materialistic views. For instance, "I love my mobile phone", instead of "I rely on my mobile phone because it helps me to be connected to the people I care about". Marketing has used 'love' as a tool to manipulate us into desiring and wanting things even if we don't really need them, and programmed us into believing that we need stuff to be loved.

There are many attachments hanging off love that we can talk about, but these are not the true essence of love, they are just side effects of genuine love. We attach love to many different things: 'If you love me, you will do what I expect of you or treat me in a specific way.' 'If I do not give many Christmas gifts, I am not showing love for my children.' 'If you love me, you will be physically intimate with me.'

Instead of just loving we are attaching expectations and terms to our love.

We have got love back to front! We have become disconnected with ourselves and seek something outside to connect with, to give us the feeling of being connected to love.

However, we are in a world that easily shows us the opposite of love because we are so emotionally disconnected from ourselves, our families, and our communities.

Love is on the inside of us and can never be found on the outside.

We deeply seek connection to others which is why social media and mobile phones are so important to us.

It is also why family is so important, yet we still don't feel as if we are loved within our families.

We keep seeking love outside when the only place it can ever be found is within us.

We have lost the skill to connect within ourselves, sometimes I wonder if this is one of the purposes of the earth plane, to learn to connect to our love.

4 – What Is Love?

Love is not how much you can give, nor how much you can touch.

It's not how much you can provide or how much you are given.

Love is not physical, but we can express our love through touch and intimacy.

To love is not about male or female. It is about our soul being accepted in our body.

Our children are our mirrors and thus loving them is loving ourselves. The love you feel for a child is simply a reflection of the love you feel for yourself - even if you doubt it.

It is a statement of trusting ourselves to be able to be at peace within ourselves and to then offer love to others, giving them that same feeling of being trusted and at peace within.

If we are showing love to the outside world through the love we are accepting in ourselves, then we are opening our souls so that the love we are showing is going to become far greater - it is going to be Universal.

Love is not something that one can learn to give like we learn to drive a car. It must be accepted and acknowledged as a part of our existence. Even the walls of your house can benefit from being loved; as can the road you drive on, and the car you drive. The trees and the plants, all things on earth, even if we deem them dead or not alive, are a living energy and can be loved.

It is not the outcome of love that is important, but the fact that you are able to love, able to accept yourself enough to give love, and to be courageous enough to seek to know the love you have within your body.

Love is not a thing that you do; it is who you are.

You are love; I am love; we are all love.

The walls are love, the chairs and tables are love, the cups are love, the marble cake with cream cheese icing is love, and the coffee is love. (I am writing in a coffee shop!)

All the love in the universe is inside us.

We can use this love to help heal others through being connected to the love that is inside and through knowing that all healing is self-healing.

All love is self-love!

We have the opportunity of helping people heal by just loving ourselves first and then letting our love love them too.

When we allow ourselves to love ourselves, we allow love to come to us.

5 - **How to Show Love**

Empower yourself as a healer by working towards 100% acknowledgment of the love that you are and you start to glow. You can then share that glow with the world. When you are full of love and power you will exude love and power everywhere, you will shine on the world, and this energy that is blossoming, overflowing and shining is the love that you give away.

Holding your power within and sharing the overflow will make you a powerful healer. It means you have the power to create change, and won't get depleted from healing. Your power level won't drop while you are healing because you are sharing the overflow and are always full and in your power.

The process of accessing your physical, mental and energetic healing brings you to the point of being at one with your own power, at one with your own love. Holding it, protecting it, and sharing the effect of self-connection is what makes an efficient healer. Using all the skills I have offered you and being gentle and kind to yourself is the way forward to being a better and more powerful healer.

Let your light shine.

I never give my power to anyone, or rather I try not to give my power to anyone. My kids can trigger me into giving in to their needs, I think it's quite normal to give in to them occasionally, ok more than occasionally, but as a healer and with most other people I never ever give away my power.

It is so easy to give out love to others, it's so easy as a healer just to kccp giving and giving, your clients are coming to receive, so it's easy just to give. Many healers and parents become exhausted by their giving, but there is a differentiation between 'giving out love' and allowing the overflow of your love to benefit others – what I term 'showing' your love.

Holding your power within and sharing the overflow makes you a powerful healer, it means you have the power within you to create change. You will not get depleted from healing, nor get drained or feel hurt after many healing sessions. Your power won't drop as you will be sharing the overflow so will always be full and always within your power.

The process of accessing your physical, mental and energetic healing brings you to the point of being at one with your own power, at one with your own love. Holding it, protecting it, and sharing the effect of self-connection, is what makes an efficient healer. Using all the skills I have offered you and being gentle and kind to yourself is the way forward to being a better and more powerful healer.

Let your light shine.

6 - All Healing is Self-Healing

This is an important core belief for me, if you want to help people through your healing ability, you also have to focus on self-healing. Although, as you are offering healing, you are receiving the healing first, it is also your responsibility to work on your personal healing and path.

How can the same clients keep coming to you if you do not shift and move and grow? You and your clients need you to work on yourself. Every single session I hold adds to and broadens my bank of healing ability from which I can draw.

It really becomes easy for you to work on yourself when you are aware that your clients are coming to you and projecting on you. When you become aware that you are being affected by their projections, you have a doorway into self-healing. As soon as you can feel and observe that you are being influenced by a client's belief, that is work for you to do on yourself. It may lead to realizations of the deepest beliefs, or it may just be a brief realization and take seconds to work through.

I have found that whatever I am going through in my life will be the issues that my clients wish to work on in their lives. Like attracts like. They were dealing with the same issues I was coping with. Because of them, I learned how to heal myself, and in return, I helped them open up to change.

When it comes down to it, your clients are paying you to heal yourself, and in return, your healing becomes their healing.

7 - Trusting Your Intuition

Firstly, you need to be as connected to yourself as you are able, allowing space within your body and mind to receive inspiration from your guides, higher self and help-ers, whoever they may be.

Secondly, once you have received the intuition, you do what you 'have' to do, and say what you 'have' to say - doing and saying mindfully, as nicely and as gently as you can, always keeping in mind that you might be completely wrong!

Distinguishing between inspiration and your mind, and being influenced by your own beliefs and needs can be tricky. When I help healers to master this skill, I tell them not to work out whether it is inspiration or their own mind, but just to trust, that it is intuition. It's easier to deal with being wrong than to stay in doubt for eternity.

If you are wrong and your client does not agree with you, or what you intuitively thought might be a cause is not, then you just go back to waiting and opening a space for more inspiration. The more you practice this without beating yourself up, the more accurate you will get and the faster it will come.

We have to start trusting ourselves at some point let go of self-doubt and accept our fear of being wrong. Being wrong is the learning tool of becoming right, so welcome being wrong in your life as a great opportunity to learn.

The easiest way for me to help you with how to trust your intuition is to tell you stories of where I have trusted my intuition and what I have learned from it.

Advanced Booking

One day I was booking a client into a time slot when I was told intuitively to keep that time for a regular client. Three days later that regular called, and I was able to tell her that I had a 6 pm appointment booked for her already!

This experience makes me smile when I think about it - a healing moment that was totally out of my control that took place outside a healing session.

Involuntary Connection

My cousin came to visit for a weekend a few months after my son was born. We were eating Sunday morning brunch in a pub when I suddenly realised that through my intuition I had reached out and pushed my finger into the back of my cousin's shoulder and she was just sitting there with her head bent forward enjoying the feeling of the connection. When I stopped, she looked at me and said that she had been in terrible pain all over her back. She had already been to a chiropractor, a physiotherapist, and a masseur but hadn't been able to tell them where the pain was coming from and they hadn't been able to solve the problem. Randomly, out of my control, I had pressed my finger on the exact place that was causing the pain. A few days later she contacted me to say that she was now totally pain-free.

The Strange Case of a Man's Chest

I was offering my time and abilities to a children's charity at a fund-raising Spiritual Fayre by seeing clients for 20-minute sessions. It was in and out, in and out, one after another. As a woman was leaving and a man was stepping in, I was completely drawn to the energetics of his chest bone, just between the solar plexus and heart chakras. The words fell out of my mouth: "What's stuck in your chest?" The man gave a huge sigh and I could see frustration falling away from his body. He told me that he had been aware that something was stuck in his chest for years. He had been to doctors and healers, anyone who might help him understand why he felt as if he needed to pull something out of his chest. Most people thought he was imagining it and he had begun to wonder if he was perhaps losing his mind. I was the first person to see that there was indeed something stuck in his chest.

I got him onto the healing couch, ran my hands over his chest then waited to find out what my guides might tell me. I received the information almost immediately. They said that when we are protecting ourselves around a trauma, we sometimes create an energetic shell that holds the trauma. After we have dealt with the trauma, the shell can sometimes get left behind. Caught in the auric field, it can block chakras, and cause pain as well as other issues, but that it wouldn't take much to release. I reached into his auric field and pulled out the stuck energy at which point he took a deep, involuntary breath, his body energy begging to realign itself.

If I had not trusted myself and had not been willing to be wrong, then I would never have allowed myself to see what he needed, even before he had asked for it. Another interesting point to make from this is that this client is still sending me clients. His belief in me and passion about his own healing helps me to help other people.

Pain Referral

Early on in my career when I was still working almost blindly, a young man of 75 years-old came to see me. He told me that only two years before he had been able to run up the stairs faster than the elevator. That he was seeing me very much against his own beliefs because he was strictly a doctors' man. However, they hadn't been able to help with his hip pain. Two years before, standing on a ladder fitting a new light bulb to the outside of his house, the ladder slipped and he began to fall. In a split second, he had to decide what to do and jumped to avoid being impaled on a post. Landing hard on his feet, he experienced an instant pain in his right hip. The doctors had used every test, scan, x-ray, and drug they could think of, but nothing had worked and he was hoping that someone weird like me would be able to help him.

We got him onto the healing couch and I connected to his hips with my hands and my awareness. After a few minutes, I became rather bored as it felt like nothing was happening. (I know now that when nothing is happening, it's because there is nothing to work on in that area). As I sat there getting lost in my awareness, I felt the urge to move my right hand up his body towards his back. I allowed it to stray, then brought it back. It pulled me to his upper back again. I felt a need to touch his spine further up and asked if he would mind turning over for me to check his back which he did, slowly and in pain.

I ran my hands through his aura a few inches above his body, hoping that somehow I would realise something and get some kind of message as to why I was doing this. I was drawn to push my fingers into his back just below his shoulder blades. With my pointing and middle fingers spread apart, I firmly pressed them on his back either side of his spine. He responded immediately, "That's the pain! That's the pain!" He was stunned that I was recreating the pain by pressing high up his back rather than on his hips. He asked me why and I replied quite calmly that it was most probably referred pain from those muscles down into the hip. I suggested he get some spine x-rays and get his doctor or a chiropractor to sort it out.

In fact, I was amazed. Stunned by what had just happened, I was simply holding it together as if I knew what I was doing when the only thing I really knew how to do was **trust my intuition**. Later I heard that once the doctors had helped him with his back, he was doing much better and getting fit again. Sometimes the most obvious, common-sense things are missed entirely.

Shoulder Out of Place

Many years ago, a client in her early sixties came to see me because of a recurring pain in her right shoulder and neck, which also went up into her face and jaw. She had had one surgery on her neck and shoulder, and two dental surgeries on her jaw and teeth to try to relieve the shooting pains. She would get the pain and have it for weeks; then it would go away of its own accord, but without warning, it could be back anytime.

I sat with my hands on her shoulders, looking down her body for a few moments to connect more deeply. My intuition was to press my right pointing finger into her right shoulder and as I did this, I could feel her react. I sat back and just looked at her body - not really in control. I mean I didn't know why I had stopped - until I noticed that her right shoulder was about two fingers higher than her left shoulder. I had been looking at bodies for a while but had never seen one side so different from the other. All of a sudden I asked her if there was a possibility that she might have slightly dislocated her shoulder known as a subluxation. I pushed on her right shoulder and it released and dropped slightly. Then I ended the session with extensive repair healing on her shoulder and her face and we agreed on another session the following week. The next day she sent me an email telling me she was pain-free.

At her next session, I gave her more remedial healing and energy balancing. What was most interesting was that when her mum had heard about the session, she had not been surprised because she remembered that when my client was a young girl she had dislocated her right shoulder at least three times and the doctors had said she would grow out of it as her body grew.

A few months later the lady returned because her shoulder was out but she had worked out that carrying her heavy grandchildren on her right hip had caused it. As I worked on her releasing the muscles to accept the shoulder back in its place she mentioned that her head was hurting, I kept on working on the shoulder, asking if the head pain had gone, but it hadn't. At the end of the session, I said: "I can't work out why the head pain didn't go away once the shoulder had released again." She replied saying "Oh, I forgot to tell you that I fell off my bicycle and hit my head on a concrete floor last week." You can't trust your clients! She has since refrained from carrying her grandchildren around any longer and now wears a helmet when cycling.

Clearing Outworn Negative Beliefs

My intuition has led me to discover that the strongest way to link to clients physically is by connecting to their base chakra through the hip joint with my left hand while putting my right hand on their shoulder which holds its own dynamic energy. This tunes me straight into the client's body flow, which in turn gives me the opportunity to hear their body much more clearly.

With this ability and the awareness that what I am most likely going to get is the client's trauma, fear or beliefs that are no longer working for them, I have established a simple way of clearing them.

I ask the client to repeat the belief I have heard from their body over and over again. This is opposite to common releasing techniques like EFT the Emotional Freedom Technique, as I am not trying to add a positive belief into the body, but simply release an old, unproductive belief from their body.

If the client has not done any emotional work on themselves and I try and add positive beliefs into the body, it creates a point of confusion - a conflict of the same belief energy. But if the client is repeating the negative belief out loud, their brain hears and acknowledges this belief, creating a space for the subconscious to become aware of this belief's traumatic effect on its own body and thus can start to make changes if they are needed. As the body starts to acknowledge the belief, it seems to increase the energy that it is focusing on the belief and becomes more active in the base chakra. This is where I am connected to with my left hand**, I feel it and grab hold of it and pull on it to release it from the body's energy field.**

8 – The Call of the Soul

When I am working with a client, I am listening to them not only with my ears but with my entire physical, emotional and soul body - all the while staying open intuitively – which enables me to hear the needs for which their bodies are screaming.

It has become clear to me that the soul calls out its trauma via the body because it cannot reach us via our minds; and if we do not listen, it will continue to increase its cry using extreme dis-ease, pain or illness. The soul is simply trying to assist the mind to evolve to a place of harmony; assisting us to replace negative thinking with positive thinking; to replace fear, mistrust, sadness, and disappointment, with love, trust, joy, and gratitude. As humans, we seem bent on focussing on the very elements that can hurt us emotionally and physically.

A WORD ON INTUITION

This has been the most amusing part of writing this book because as my editor pointed out this book on intuitive healing has no information on how to become more intuitive!

Many of the tools I offer in the book are designed to make it easier for your intuition to flow and improve, but it is not possible for me to address your particular intuitive abilities without meeting you in person. Yes, you have intuition, and yes your intuition can help you in your life as a human and as a healer, but it is up to you to discover and develop it yourself. What I can tell you is that your intuition is in your gut and soul and in your humanity. It is not in your thinking mind and thinking ability, although your thinking ability can be used to observe your instinctive feelings and process the observations into understanding using your left/right brain balance.

Intuition for healing is all about trusting your instinct. When using your intuition for healing, trust what feels right in your body. The little pushes, the little twitches, the itch on your leg, even the frustration you may feel with a client. Each time I have to trust what my instinct tells me. Sometimes my finger feels the need to move just a tiny amount for me to be on the right spot; sometimes I want to move and move and move the energy around a person's stomach, and so I start to massage it.

Intuition is very delicate and subtle at first, but you have to have the courage to jump into what you think you might be feeling and go for it and allow yourself to be wrong. Let yourself dive off the edge of the cliff and trust the subtle little thing you may have felt. Rest assured that as time goes by and you become more and more used to the subtleness, it will become clearer and clearer. These days my intuition can be so clear that it is like being hit by a bus and some-times it comes so fast that my brain is unable to hold on to it. As it flashes through I have to slow myself down and then go into reverse, hoping that I get it again. Happily, I usually do.

As you develop your intuitive talent, you will find that you also develop a unique, intuitive language. It might be with your higher self, through spirit communication, psy-chic ability (energy reading), Clair-cognisance (a universal knowing), shamanic contact, or perhaps something no-one else has ever seen before. An important lesson to learn is that your intuition is not comparable to anyone else's intui-tion. You must never ever compare yourself to others - we are too individual for comparison, but that does not mean you cannot learn from other people's abilities. I am often in awe of the way other people show their intuition.

A young 18-year-old with learning difficulties attends my healing development group with her Dad. Everyone in the group not only enjoys her uniqueness but is in awe of the accuracy of her intuition. When you see past her wanting to hug you all the time, let go of her burping and giggling and locking herself in the toilet all the time and see who she is when she is healing, you would be amazed. She sits there in her individuality that often looks very 'special needs' and the words and the intuition and the knowing that comes from her is outstanding, exciting and incredibly accurate.

When teaching intuitive development in groups I ask each person to explain the symbolism they intuit from an item or an idea. In suggesting "A black and orange butterfly sitting on a leaf," one group member might say "Butterflies live for a short time, so sit down and enjoy your time." Another might say "The orange of the butterfly is a sign of the sacral chakra, so sit down and focus on your trauma." Someone else might say "The butterfly symbolises meta-morphosis, so sit down and allow for change." My own view is that the butterfly symbolises the end of the old and the beginning of the new – both reflecting the life span of the butterfly, and the black and orange colours. A sign to allow changes to happen in your life even if you feel as if you are not going to get through them; and to wait for life to bring the changes - as you haven't got a choice - and that the outcome will be a life full of joy, harmony and one in which your dreams will come to fruition. So all members of the group are able to learn from the different points of view which they are free to accept or reject. Hence there is no comparing - only learning.

Some time ago, a gentleman who wanted to join one of my intuitive learning groups was afraid he wouldn't 'fit in'. He told me that he seemed unable to make the same sort of spiritual connections as other people and had been shunned from other groups and a spiritual church. And at his first meeting he had found it a little difficult to follow our way of doing things. The following week I simply asked him, "Who are you drawn to?" He hesitated, afraid of being wronged or rejected, and then said: "I am drawn to that lady." When I asked him "Why?" he replied eagerly, "She has an eagle with her, and that means.........and "That man over there has a seagull, and that means........." He ended up going around the entire group with extreme enthusiasm explaining what birds or animals he saw.

We are all individual and so must grow our intuition independently through self-awareness and self-acceptance.

The best way to learn more about your unique intuition is to do healing, join groups, play with it, use it, and to let go of any negative uncertainty you are holding. Get it into your mind that to become more intuitive you have to be willing to get it wrong thousands of times before you are comfortable getting it right all the time.

IN CONCLUSION

Thank you for reading this book, I want to tell you that it takes practice and patience to become the true powerful healer that you are. And even then, when you get there it will only just be the beginning of your development. I believe if I can do it in my way, you can do it in your way.

I believe we are all intuitive and we all can find away to help ourselves and others, some of us have been given these tools as children but many of us need to learn them as we go along. In the face of self-doubt and uncertainty, I ask you to trust your gut, trust the deepest part of you and go for it. Go for it with all of your soul and give yourself across as calmly, gently and lovingly as you can. Any healing you offer is healing yourself. Never give up on yourself, our world needs the healing.

Thank you...

Milton Keynes UK
Ingram Content Group UK Ltd.
UKHW020751061123
432055UK00019B/876

9 781999 963019